NARCISSISM

AND

ENTANGLEMENT

A guide on healing from the scars, restoring your faith in love

Shakeerah Arrignton

This document is geared towards providing exact and reliable information with regards to the topic and issue covered. The publication is sold with the idea that the publisher is not required to render accounting, officially permitted, or otherwise, qualified services. If advice is necessary, legal or professional, a practiced individual in the profession should be ordered.

- From a Declaration of Principles which was accepted and approved equally by a Committee of the American Bar Association and a Committee of Publishers and Associations.

In no way is it legal to reproduce, duplicate, or transmit any part of this document in either electronic means or in printed format. Recording of this publication is strictly prohibited and any storage of this document is not allowed unless with written permission from the publisher. All rights reserved.

The information provided herein is stated to be truthful and consistent, in that any liability, in terms of inattention or otherwise, by any usage or abuse of any policies, processes, or directions contained within is the solitary and utter responsibility of the recipient reader. Under no circumstances will any legal responsibility or blame be held against the publisher for any reparation, damages, or monetary loss due to the information herein, either directly or indirectly.

Respective authors own all copyrights not held by the publisher.

The information herein is offered for informational purposes solely, and is universal as so. The presentation of the information is without contract or any type of guarantee assurance.

The trademarks that are used are without any consent, and the publication of the trademark is without permission or backing by the trademark owner. All trademarks and brands within this book are for clarifying purposes only and are the owned by the owners themselves, not affiliated with this document

Contents

DEDICATION

For my awesome children Sincere, Jordyn, Christian, and Taylen. You all are my world. Remember, anything you believe, you can achieve.

INTRODUCTION

In our lifetime, we are all members of a few families: the one that we are born to and the one(s) that we make. We all pass from the former to the latter hurts, attitudes, fears, expectations and aspirations-an entire emotional baggage. No exception is the narcissist.

The narcissist has a dichotomous view of humanity: either humans are sources of narcissistic supply (and, therefore, idealized and over-valued) or they do not serve this purpose (and are thus useless, devalued). The narcissist obtains from himself all the love he desires. He requires acceptance, validation, respect, adoration, affection from the outside-in other words, the externalized boundary functions of the Ego.

He does not need-and does not pursue-the love of his parents or his siblings, or to be loved by his children. He casts them in the theatre of his exaggerated grandiosity as the audience. He wants to impress them, to shock them, to intimidate them, to infuse them with reverence, to inspire them, to draw their attention, to subjugate or to exploit them. This book is part of a series that describes the abuse of narcissism in great detail. Enjoy the below pages.

CHAPTER ONE

NARCISSIST – MEANING AND COMPONENTS

Someone who is a true narcissist varies in ways from just the typical self-centered person (who may be obnoxiously narcissistic, but falls short of a psychiatric diagnosis), in other words, who suffers from Narcissistic Personality Disorder (NPD). NPD is described by the Mayo Clinic as "a mental disorder in which individuals have an exaggerated sense of their own importance, a profound need for excessive recognition and admiration, troubled relationships, and a lack of empathy for others." People with NPD appear to have a skewed self-image and are deeply concerned with themselves, contributing to the lack of empathy. Research indicates that less than 1 percent of the population is affected by NPD, and that 50-75% of those who have it are males.

What are a narcissist's characteristics?

- People with NPD expect to undergo special counseling.
- They exaggerate their smarts, popularity, wealth, and looks of their own.
- The lack of empathy leads them, with no remorse, to take advantage of others.
- There might be intensely jealous and ultra-sensitive narcissists.
- Since they appear to be very thin-skinned, at any criticism or push-back, they can angrily lash out.
- When they feel like they're not getting special treatment, narcissists can even lash out.

A strong sense of vulnerability is behind all of these traits.

And, no big surprise, narcissists can find it super-difficult to have healthy relationships and have tons of trouble at work or school when you consider all these characteristics.

The Family and The Narcissist

In our lifetime, we are all members of a few families: the one that we are born to and the one(s) that we make. We all pass from the former to the latter hurts, attitudes, fears, expectations and aspirations-an entire emotional baggage. No exception is the narcissist.

The narcissist has a dichotomous view of humanity: either humans are sources of narcissistic supply (and, therefore, idealized and over-valued) or they do not serve this purpose (and are thus useless, devalued). The narcissist obtains from himself all the love he desires. He requires acceptance, validation, respect, adoration, affection from the outside-in other words, the externalized boundary functions of the Ego.

He does not need-and does not pursue-the love of his parents or his siblings, or to be loved by his children. He casts them in the theatre of his exaggerated grandiosity as the audience. He wants to impress them, to shock them, to intimidate them, to infuse them with reverence, to inspire them, to draw their attention, to subjugate or to exploit them.

He emulates and simulates a whole spectrum of feelings and uses every means to achieve these results. He lies (pathological liars are narcissists-a false one is their own self). The pitiful, or, on the contrary, the resilient and effective, actions. He stuns and shines with excellent intellectual, or physical skill and successes, or patterns of behaviour valued by family members. The narcissist is likely to go through three stages when faced with (younger) siblings or with his own children:

He perceives his offspring or siblings at first as a danger to his narcissistic supply, such as his spouse's or mother's attention, as the case may be. They penetrate the Pathological Narcissistic Domain and intrude on his turf. The narcissist tries his utmost to discredit them, damage them (even physically) and humiliate them, and then he retreats into an imagined realm of omnipotence when these reactions prove counterproductive or counterproductive. There follows a time of emotional absence and separation.

The narcissist continues to indulge himself in daydreaming, fantasies of grandeur, plotting of potential coups, longing and hurt (the Lost Paradise Syndrome), his violence having failed to evoke Narcissistic Supply. This is how the narcissist responds to the birth of his children or the introduction of new attention to the family cell (even to a new pet!).

Whoever perceives the narcissist as competing for scarce narcissistic supplies is relegated to the enemy's position. The narcissist tends to stay away if the uninhibited expression of the aggression and hostility aroused by this predicament is unconstitutional or unlikely. He often suddenly disconnects, detaches himself mentally, becomes cold and uninterested, or directs transformed rage at his partner or his parents (the more "legitimate" targets) rather than targeting his offspring or siblings.

In the 'mishap,' other narcissists see the chance. They attempt to exploit their parents by "taking over" the newcomer (or their mate). Their siblings or their unborn children are monopolised by such narcissists. This way, they profit indirectly from the attention directed at the infants. The sibling or offspring become the narcissist's vicarious sources of narcissistic supply and proxies.

An example: A narcissistic father secures the grateful affection of the mother by being closely associated with his offspring ("What an excellent father / brother he is"). He also takes part or all of the credit for the successes of the baby / sibling. This is a method of the other's annexation and assimilation, a technique that the narcissist uses in most of his encounters.

The narcissist starts to see their ability to be edifying, reliable and adequate sources of narcissistic supply as siblings or offspring grow older. His mindset, then, is changed fully. The previous threats have now become future promises. He cultivates the most rewarding those he trusts to be. He inspires them to idolize him, to adore him, to be afraid of him, to respect his actions and skill, to learn to trust and follow him blindly, to submit to his charm in short, and to be absorbed in his folly-de-grandeur.

The risk of child abuse-up to and including outright incest-is increased at this point. Auto-erotic is the narcissist. He is his own sexual attraction's chosen object. His genetic material is shared by his siblings and his children. Molesting or having intercourse with them is as close to having sex with himself as the narcissist gets.

In addition, in terms of annexation, the narcissist perceives sex. The partner is "assimilated" and becomes an extension, a completely controlled and manipulated entity, of the narcissist. To the narcissist, sex is the final act of the other's depersonalization and objectification. Currently, he masturbates with the bodies of other people.

Minors face no risk of criticising or questioning the narcissist. They are ideal sources of Narcissistic Supply, maleable and plentiful. The narcissist derives pleasure from making coital interactions with inferior, inexperienced and dependent "bodies" adulating, physically and mentally.

These tasks-delegated to them by the narcissist directly and demandingly or indirectly and perniciously-are better performed by those whose mind is not yet completely developed and autonomous. The older the siblings or heirs, the more critical of the narcissist, even judgmental, they become. They are better able to bring his acts into sense and perspective, to challenge his motivations, to predict his movements.

When they mature, the mindless pawns in their chess game frequently fail to continue to play. They keep grudges against him for what he did to them in the past, when they were less resilient. They will calculate his true height, abilities, and accomplishments-which are typically far behind the statements he makes.

This takes the narcissist back to the first stage for a complete loop. He perceives his brothers or sons/daughters as threats again. He is easily disillusioned and devalued. He loses all interest, becomes distant, absent and cold emotionally, refuses any attempt to engage with him, citing the demands of life and the preciousness and scarcity of his time.

He feels burdened, besieged, cornered, smothered, and claustrophobic. He wants to get free, to give up his responsibilities to people who have become utterly worthless (or even harmful) to him. He doesn't understand why he has to help them, or to suffer from their company, and he feels he's been purposely and ruthlessly caught.

Either passively-aggressively (by refusing to act or deliberately sabotaging relationships) or actively (by being excessively critical, hostile, unpleasant, abusive verbally and mentally, etc.), he rebels. Slowly-to explain his conduct to himself-he gets immersed in strong delusional hues in conspiracy theories.

The family members conspire against him in his view, attempt to belittle or humiliate or subordinate him, do not understand him, or stymie his growth. Typically, the narcissist eventually gets what he wants and the family he has built disintegrates to his great sorrow (due to the loss of the Narcissistic Space) -but also to his great relief and surprise (how could someone as special as him have been let go?).

This is the cycle: the narcissist feels threatened by the introduction of new family members-he attempts to assimilate or annex siblings or offspring-he obtains narcissistic supplies from them-he overestimates and idealizes these new sources-as sources grow older and autonomous, they adopt anti-narcissistic attitudes-the narcissist devalues them-the narcissist feels stifled and trapped-the narcissist feels stifled and trapped

This cycle characterizes not just the narcissist's family life. In other realms of his life (his work, for example), it is to be found. The narcissist, initially, feels threatened at work (nobody knows him, nobody is him). Then, in order to receive narcissistic supplies from them, he establishes a network of admirers, cronies and friends that he "nurtures and cultivates." He overestimates them (they are the brightest, the most loyal to him, with the greatest chances of ascending the corporate ladder and other superlatives).

But the narcissist devalues all these previously idealized individuals after some anti-narcissistic actions on their part (a critical comment, a dispute, a rejection, however polite) They are judged by him to be dumb, cowardly, lacking in motivation, abilities and skills, popular (the worst expletive in the narcissist's vocabulary), with an unspectacular future ahead of them, now that they have dared to oppose him.

The narcissist believes that his limited and invaluable resources (for example, his time) are misallocated by him. He feels besieged, he feels suffocated. In a series of self-defeating and self-destructive actions that lead to the disintegration of his life, he rebels and erupts.

In his "death wish," the narcissist is predictable, destined to create and destroy, connect and remove, enjoy and depreciate. What sets him apart from other suicidal forms is that, in his anguished life, his desire is given to him in small, tormenting doses.

CHAPTER TWO

ORIGINS

Clinical theories of narcissism, such as those of the Austrian psychoanalysts Heinz Kohut and Otto Kernberg, posit that early childhood experiences have their origins in adult narcissism. In early social (parental) relationships, both Kohut and Kernberg concentrate on disruptions as the genesis of adult narcissistic personality disorder. Also, at its heart, both perceive narcissism as a failure in the creation of a healthy self. According to Kohut, through experiences with others (primarily the mother) that give the child opportunities to gain acceptance and enhancement and to connect with ideal and omnipotent role models, the child's self grows and gains maturity. In two ways, parents who are empathic lead to the balanced growth of the child's self. Second, they have mirroring that fosters a sense of self that is more rational. Second, parents expose in themselves shortcomings that lead the child to internalize or believe an idealized picture that can be true and attainable. When the parent is unempathetic and fails to provide approval and suitable role models, issues are introduced. Narcissism, according to Kohut, is in fact a developmental arrest, a halt in the development of the child at what was a natural and necessary level, leading to the grandiose and unrealistic self of the child. At the same time, in order to preserve self-esteem by comparison, the child continues to idealize others.

Kernberg's theory, by contrast, argues that narcissism is a defense. This results from the reaction of the child to coldness and lack of empathy on the part of the parents, likely resulting from their own narcissism. The child becomes emotionally hungry, according to Kernberg, and reacts to the parents' negligence with frustration. The narcissistic defense in this view represents the attempt of the child to take refuge in some part of self that evokes admiration in others, a defense that eventually results in a grandiose and exaggerated sense of self. In Kernberg's opinion, narcissists are grandiose on the outside, but fragile on the inside, challenging their self-worth.

Kernberg and Kohut's theories both describe narcissists as people with a childhood history of unsatisfactory social interactions who have grandiose expectations of themselves as adults that encourage a contradictory psychological dependency on others.

Behavior And Narcissistic Pathology

The NPI's research findings depict a picture of narcissists as having exaggerated and grandiose self-images. It is also not shocking that narcissists report that they have high self-esteem. These optimistic self-images, however, seem to be founded on skewed and exaggerated views of their successes and their distorted impressions about what others think of them. They overestimate their physical attractiveness, for example, in relation to judges' ratings of their attractiveness, and overestimate their intelligence in relation to objective IQ tests. In one experiment, a woman whose answers were scripted was interviewed by narcissistic and nonnarcissistic men (as defined on the basis of their NPI results), so all the men received the same social input. The narcissistic men, however, judged the attraction of the woman to them more strongly than nonnarcissistic men did. Other studies suggest that even though such results happened by luck or chance, narcissists take greater credit for positive results.

While the self-esteem of narcissists is strong, it is also fragile and uncertain, as demonstrated by its variability. From moment to moment, day to day, it fluctuates more than less-narcissistic individuals. Other research shows that narcissists are more likely to have high explicit self-esteem (conscious, self-reported) and low implicit self-esteem (non-conscious, or automatic). This result indicates that their unconscious feelings about themselves are not so positive, even though narcissists describe themselves in positive terms.

The optimistic yet insecure self-views of narcissists lead them to be more attentive and receptive to other individuals' input. However, for narcissists, not just any reaction or input from others is important; they are eager to learn that others respect them and look up to them. Rather than being liked and embraced, narcissists admire respect and dominance. Studies found that the self-esteem of narcissists depends on the degree to which they feel respected. In addition, narcissists seek admiration from others by trying to exploit others' impressions. They make self-promoting and self-aggrandizing comments and try to ask others around them for consideration and compliments. When they feel threatened by others, they also respond with rage and resentment. In such occasions, they are more likely to react violently and derogate those who challenge them, even though such hostile responses jeopardize the relationship.

Narcissists try to solicit admiration from others around them, and their aggression adds to the disturbed interpersonal relationships that are a characteristic of the condition when others fail to react appropriately. Research has shown that by boasting and putting down others, people describe their narcissistic acquaintances as trying to please others. These habits are initially effective in making them competent and appealing to others who associate with narcissists. However, these partners come to consider the narcissist as vain and aggressive over time.

Findings from a number of research indicate an image of narcissists as individuals who use their friends to feel good about themselves. To endorse self-images that are optimistic yet easily challenged, they pander for praise and appreciation. For even the slightest slight that they interpret as disrespect, they are constantly on warning. Perhaps most important, the striving of narcissists to self-enhance at the cost of

Ultimately, their mates lost them friendships.

Narcissist: The High Functioning one

When it comes to a man who stays out all night, drinks, uses narcotics, obviously has affairs, is reckless with money, can't hold a job, and shows both verbal and physical violence at home, it's easy to spot violence. It is possible to mark or diagnose men with these kinds of traits as having narcissistic personality disorder because they take no responsibility for their actions or how it affects others in their lives. While their lives look chaotic from the point of view of the partners, the narcissistic personality covers his actions by ignoring it and concentrating instead on his partner's faults. While this kind of narcissist may be a total and complete failure in the real world, he is destined for grandeur in his fantasy world and uses promises and a fantastic sales presentation to keep his partner hooked. But the partner starts to understand that she can't create a life on false promises and initiates change after several years have passed and nothing changes.

The story is entirely different for the high-functioning narcissist. In the real world, he is always very responsible, has a decent career, owns his own company, has good money management, has good credit, owns his own house, is highly intelligent and imaginative, may have long-term marriage or relationship histories, is involved with his children, takes excellent physical care of himself and may also be an influential member of society, the church, or involved in individuals

For a highly functioning narcissist, violence and instability are difficult to detect. In reality, partners of this kind of narcissistic personality often believe that they are the issue. And if there is an extra-marital affair for the highly functioning narcissist, he would make his wife believe she forced him to do it. Often it is also the narcissist's wife that is led to have an affair because at home she is not having her needs met. This is not shocking, because her needs are not important to him, regardless of his appearance in society. They are simply a total annoyance.

They are continually outsmarting and even brainwashing their partners while interacting with these extremely intelligent, highly functioning narcissistic personalities, re-enforcing the suggestion that the partner is the one with the problem. The wife is experiencing energy loss, personal power loss, deteriorating self-worth, and eventually the loss of her ability to work in the world. She has lost her hold on reality entirely and has been absorbed into the reality of narcissism. Normally, once the partnership has fallen apart, she comes to the conclusion that her spouse is narcissistic. By this time, as the former wife clearly did not, she was mostly already replaced by someone he considered to be "getting her act together." This just adds to her emotions of worthlessness.

This is the contrast between a personality that is narcissistic and one that is not. A narcissist can't put his partners in their shoes. On the other side of the situation, he can't imagine what it would feel like to be. He can see it only from his own viewpoint, which is a viewpoint that totally lets him off the hook and places 100% of the blame on his partner.

CHAPTER THREE

NARCISSISM: A DESTRUCTIVE TRAIL OF DECEIT

Today's narcissists crowd our planet. They are our wives, our former wives, our families, our superiors, our colleagues, our spiritual mentors, our mates. With money, recognition, adulation, celebrity, and social standing, our society rewards narcissists handsomely. The raison d'etre of the narcissist is winning. Nothing else matters as long as he achieves his goals. Personal concerns are too intricate, messy and time consuming, including those of close family members. As people with this personality disorder are ethically and morally challenged, this ensures that the narcissistic uses are inconsequential. The narcissist often drives in the fast lane with his grandiose sense of self-entitlement and no confined attitude.

Narcissists weave grand illusions of achievement designed to lead them to riches, authority, reputation, and power stashes. The narcissist is electrified by winning; it is the engine, the fire, which keeps him going. These people are also creative in their knowledge of creative goods and services and how to market them effectively. They recruit bright creative individuals to execute their ideas. Narcissists are also virtuosos of the big picture who leave to others the nuances and hard work. By underpaying them and overpromising, they take advantage of their subordinates while carefully preserving their elite lifestyles. The written or verbal arrangement with a narcissist that you make is never the actual contract. The narcissist realizes that, as long as you can get away with it, contracts can still be broken.

Above all, in all of his partnerships and transactions, the narcissist is dishonest. With automatic ease, he bends the facts. Members of the inner circle of the narcissist also themselves have flawed characters. As long as it is to their material gain, they are ready and able to indulge in underhanded tactics. Low-level narcissists who lack the thinnest veneer of conscience or humanity are some assistants and hangers-on. They remain at the feet of the master narcissist, thinking they would be rubbed off by his riches and stature.

High-level narcissists — those people who are especially magnetic, brilliant, friendly, and confident — are also talented at wealth development. The "right people" are thankful to them, have impeccable timing, and know exactly how to make their moves. Not all rich people are narcissists. Many people with wealth are generous, compassionate people who are not dependent on material possessions.

Some visions of narcissism go astray. Offices are locked, workers are dumped without notice, bills, loans and leases are left unpaid when the trip becomes bumpy or the narcissist whimsically tries to change direction. Without technical or financial support, many who have entered the narcissist in good faith, even moved across the nation to become part of his team, are deserted. In extreme emotional distress, they are left to pick up bits of their shattered lives. There's an unmoved narcissist. He's not losing sleep over the debacles. He's going ahead and pivoting towards his next major project. Narcissists repeat these damaging patterns of deceit over the course of their lives.

Stop yourself from being enmeshed in the toxic net of the narcissist. Learn to recognize narcissists who enter your private and professional life. Steer clear, if you may, of them. If you are needed to communicate with a narcissist, always be aware that their aim is to win at all costs, no matter how attractive, strong, persuasive, or magnetic they are, even if that means harming others.

Codependent Narcissists

Narcissists and codependents are often distinguished by writers as opposites, but interestingly, while their outward actions can vary, they share several psychological characteristics. In reality, narcissists show core codependent symptoms of guilt, denial, power, (unconscious) dependence, and dysfunctional communication and limits, all contributing to problems with intimacy. A strong association between narcissism and codependency was shown by one study.

I While it is possible to identify most narcissists as codependents, the opposite is not true-most codependents are not narcissists. They do not show traditional exploitation, entitlement, and lack of empathy traits.

Dependence

Codependency is a "missing self" condition. Codependents have missing their attachment to their intrinsic self. Their thought and actions, instead, revolve around a person, material, or process. Narcissists suffer from a lack of interaction with their true self as well. They're associated with their ideal self in their position. They are dependent on others for affirmation because of their inner deprivation and lack of connection to their real selves. As a consequence, in order to stabilize and affirm their self-esteem and fragile ego, their self-image, thought, and actions are other-oriented, like other codependents.

Ironically, narcissists need attention from others amid proclaimed high self-regard and have an insatiable desire to be praised - to get their "narcissistic supply." This makes them as dependent on others' attention as an addict is on their addiction.

Shame

At the heart of codependency and addiction is guilt. In a broken household, it comes from growing up. Self-opinion inflated by narcissists is typically mistaken for self-love. Exaggerated self-flattery and arrogance, however, merely relieve implicit, internalized shame among codependents that is normal.

In dysfunctional households, children learn multiple ways of dealing with the fear, uncertainty, and aggression they feel growing up. Despite the good intentions of parents and the lack of overt violence, internalized shame will result. Kids adopt coping patterns to feel secure, giving rise to an ideal self. One method is to accommodate other individuals and seek their love, affection, and approval. Another is the quest for acceptance, superiority, and supremacy over others. The first group is covered by traditional codependents, and the second by narcissists. In order to get their needs met, they seek power and control over their world. They are helped to avoid feeling inferior, weak, needy, and powerless at all costs by their pursuit of prestige, dominance, and strength.

These values are normal human requirements; they are compulsive and therefore neurotic for codependents and narcissists, however. Furthermore, the more a person pursues their ideal self, the more they depart from their real self, which only increases their fear, false self, and sense of shame. (See Conquering Shame and Codependency for more on these trends and how shame and codependency co-emerge in childhood.)

Denial

A key symptom of codependency is denial. Generally, codependents are in denial of their codependency, also their thoughts and many needs. Likewise, narcissists deny emotions, particularly those that express vulnerability. Many would not admit, even to themselves, to feelings of inadequacy. We disown and sometimes project feelings that they deem "weak," such as longing, depression, loneliness, impotence, shame, fear, and variations of them, onto others. Anger makes them feel strong. Defenses against underlying humiliation are anger, greed, jealousy, and disdain.

Codependents deny their needs, especially emotional needs, which have been ignored or disgraced as they grow up. Some co-dependents are self-sufficient and put other needs first quickly. Some co-dependents need individuals to meet their needs. Emotional needs are often ignored by narcissists. They're not going to say they're demanding and needy, because having needs makes them feel vulnerable and dependent. Like the poor, they judge.

Although narcissists generally don't put other people's needs first, some narcissists are genuinely people-pleasers and can be quite compassionate. In addition to securing the attachment of those on whom they rely, since they are able to support individuals they consider inferior, their motive is also for praise or to feel superior or grandiose. They may feel abused by and resentful towards the individuals they support, like most codependents.

When it comes to needs for emotional closeness, support, grieving, nurturing, and secrecy, many narcissists hide behind a mask of self-sufficiency and aloofness. In order to escape rejection and feeling guilt, the quest for power prevents them from experiencing the embarrassment of feeling vulnerable, sad, scared, or wanting or needing someone. Only the danger of abandonment shows how dependent they really are.

Dysfunctional Frontiers

Narcissists have unhealthy limits, like other codependents, since theirs were not respected growing up. They do not view other entities as different, but as extensions of themselves. As a consequence, they project thoughts and emotions on others and blame them for their failures and errors, all of which they are unable to tolerate in themselves. In addition, the absence of constraints makes them thin-skinned, extremely emotional, and defensive, allowing them to take it all personally.

These habits of blame, reactivity, defensiveness, and taking things personally are shared by most codependents. The actions and degree or direction of feelings may differ, but there is a common underlying mechanism. Many codependents, for instance, respond with self-criticism, self-blame, or withdrawal, while others respond with someone else's hostility and criticism or blame. Yet, both acts are responses to guilt and display dysfunctional limits. (Confrontation or avoidance may be an acceptable response in certain instances, but not if it is a normal, compulsive reaction.)

Dysfunctional Connection

The interaction of narcissists is unhealthy, like other codependents. Generally, assertiveness capabilities are lacking. Criticism, requests, marking, and other types of verbal violence also consist of their contact. Some narcissists, on the other hand, intellectualize, obfuscate, and are indirect. They find it hard to define and explicitly state their emotions, like most codependents. While they can more readily express ideas and take positions than other codependents, they also have difficulty listening and are dogmatic and inflexible. These are signs of dysfunctional communication that indicate vulnerability and the other person's lack of respect.

Controlling

Narcissists want power, as other co-dependents. In order to feel safe, power over our environment helps us. The greater our depression and confusion, the greater our need for order. What people think, say, and do is paramount to our sense of well-being and even survival, because we depend on others for our survival, happiness, and self-worth. With people-pleasing, lies, or manipulation, we'll try to manipulate them directly or indirectly. We try to control our emotions if we're afraid or ashamed of our emotions, such as anger or sorrow. The rage or sorrow of other people will upset us, so they must be stopped or controlled, too.

The Intimacy

Finally, for narcissists and codependents, the mixture of all these patterns makes intimacy difficult. Relationships do not flourish without clear boundaries that offer independence and dignity to partners. They need us to be independent, to have assertive communication skills, and to have self-esteem.

CHAPTER FOUR

GENDER AND THE

NARCISSIST

Female and male narcissists, naturally, tend to differ in the expression of their narcissism. They underline numerous items. They turn various aspects of their character and of their lives into the cornerstones of their disorder.

(As they do in eating disorders: Anorexia Nervosa and Bulimia Nervosa), women focus on their body. Their physical charms, their individuality, their socially and culturally defined "femininity" are flaunted and abused. Via their more conventional gender position, they protect their narcissistic supply: home, infants, acceptable jobs, their husbands ('the wife of...'), their feminine characteristics, their position in society, etc.

It is no wonder that narcissists are chauvinistic and conservative-both male and female. They rely to such an extent on the views of the people around them that, over time, they are turned into ultra-sensitive public opinion seismographs, prevailing wind barometers and conformity guardians. Narcissists are unable to afford to severely alienate those who represent their False Selves to them. The very proper and on-going functioning of their Ego is based on their human environment's goodwill and cooperation.

True, besieged and overwhelmed by feelings of pernicious remorse-many are eventually trying to be punished by a narcissist. Then, the self-destructive narcissist plays the "bad guy" (or "bad girl") role. But it is within the conventional socially assigned positions even then. The narcissist exaggerates these positions into a caricature to guarantee social opprobrium (read: attention). A woman is likely to self-label herself a "whore" and to self-style herself a "vicious, unrepentant criminal" male narcissist. Yet, these are conventional social roles once again. Intellect, strength, violence, wealth, or social standing are likely to be emphasised by men. Women, even as they pursue their masochistic retribution, are likely to emphasize body, appearance, appearance, attractiveness, feminine "traits", homemaking, children and child rearing.

Another distinction lies in the way the sexes react to treatment. As they are more likely to confess to psychological issues, women are more likely to resort to counseling. But though men may be less likely to Confess or to reveal their issues to others (the element of macho-man)-this does not necessarily mean that they are less likely to admit it to themselves. Women are more likely than men to ask for support as well.

Nevertheless, it is never appropriate to neglect the primary law of narcissism: the narcissist uses everything around him or her to receive his or her narcissistic supply. Owing to the still existing prejudiced system of our culture and the fact that women are the ones to give birth, children happen to be more available to the female narcissist. It is easier for a woman to think of her children as her extensions because they were once her physical extensions and because they are now more intensive and more detailed in her ongoing relationship with them.

Narcissistic relations

"Numerous people email me about their unhappiness and difficulties in coping with a challenging loved one, frequently a narcissistic spouse or parent who is uncooperative, greedy, cold, and often violent, after writing" Codependency for Dummies. Narcissist partners feel torn between their love and their pain, between remaining and leaving, but they cannot seem to do anything. They feel neglected, they feel ignored,

What's Narcissistic Personality Disorder?

The term narcissism is widely used by the general public to characterize personality characteristics, usually someone who is greedy or wants attention. In reality, a degree of healthy narcissism produces a well-balanced, strong personality. On the other hand, a narcissistic personality disorder (NPD) is somewhat different and needs clear requirements to be met for a diagnosis. It only affects a small personality disorder (NPD). "One with NPD is grandiose (sometimes only in fantasy), lacks empathy, and wants other people's respect, as five of these summarized features indicate:

- A grandiose sense of self-importance that exaggerates accomplishments and abilities
- Dreams of infinite power, accomplishment, brilliance, elegance, or ideal love
- Lack of concern for others' thoughts and needs

Excessive admiration needs

- He or she claims that he or she is special and exceptional, and can only be understood by or connected with other persons (or institutions) of special or high status.
- Unique, favorable treatment or compliance with his or her wishes is unreasonably expected.
- Exploits and makes use of others in order to achieve personal ends
- Envies others or thinks that he or she is envious of them

- Has "an attitude" of superiority or the way of behaving

The disease also ranges from mild to severe. But of all the narcissists, beware of the most pernicious, aggressive, and destructive malignant narcissists. They take characteristics 6 & 7 to a severe and are vindictive and malicious. Stop them until they kill you.

Narcissists' Children

Narcissistic parents usually run the household and can damage their children's self-esteem and motivation severely. They also attempt to live through them vicariously. Such parents expect success and/or obedience, and can be competitive, envious, critical, oppressive, or needy. Although their personalities vary, the common aspect is that their emotions and needs, particularly emotor needs, are different.

Although their parents feel entitled, they feel unentitled and self-sacrificing and deny their own emotions and needs (unless they are narcissistic too). They may not learn to trust and respect themselves and grow up isolated from their true selves. They may be motivated to prove themselves in order to gain the approval of their parents, but find little incentive to fulfill their wants and aspirations when not externally

While they may be unaware of what was lacking in their adolescence, their adult relationships appear to be permeated with fear of abandonment and intimacy. They are afraid of causing waves or errors and becoming real. Many are used to finding external affirmation, pretending to feel what they don't and hiding what they do. They believe their only choice with reenacting their family drama.

Narcissistic parents' adult children are frequently depressed, have unrecognized resentment, and feelings of emptiness. They may attract an alcoholic, a narcissist, or another unavailable spouse, continuing the emotional abandonment cycle from childhood. Healing includes rehabilitation from codependency and the toxic guilt gained in a narcissistic home to resolve.

Narcissists' Partners

Narcissist partners feel deceived because as time went by, the considerate, attentive and loving person they fell in love with vanished. They feel invisible and lonely, and long for emotional interaction. They find it difficult to convey their rights, desires, and feelings in varying degrees and to set limits. The relationship reflects the emotional abandonment and sense of entitlement.

Occasionally, they receive reminders of the warmth and care of the person with whom they first fell in love, sometimes smart, imaginative, talented, popular, handsome or beautiful. They don't hesitate to claim that if only they felt more valued and respected, they are committed to remaining in the relationship. Divorce is not a choice for some people.

CHAPTER FIVE

WHY NARCISSISTIC MOTHERS HATE THEIR DAUGHTERS

It's never easy to consider living in a house where your mother is a narcissist. They hide behind someone else's façade. They're pretending to be something nicer, a decent parent to the outside world. But behind closed doors, the drama and the actual violence take place. Abused teens suffer from emotional distress, humiliation, disrespect for who they are, where they feel worthless and guilty.

As autonomous human beings, they have no right to shine and grow up with dignity.

When a girl is entering the puberty stage, it is extremely noticeable. That is why her daughter is treated more cruelly by a narcissistic mother than her son. Her mother is challenged by her youth and future, as her daughter transforms into a woman. Then, very jealous, possessive and violent, she becomes. She treats it as an extension of herself.

About why? She knows she's growing older! She knows she has missed tremendous opportunities for life, great relationships, and she is struggling with her own violence of the past. Her daughter reminds her of the painful reality of a life of her own. She is a threat to her, and she accuses her of compromising a stay-at - home mom's existence.

It is for this reason that envy comes to the surface. At every opportunity, she must leap and take all of her accumulated frustration out on her. She considers her low self-esteem and feelings of disappointment a temporary relief.

She is undermining the self-esteem and self-worth of her daughter by her abuse. That is why she is unable to grow to her full potential and satisfaction. "You have no right to be happy, free, be beautiful and successful" is the secret message to her.

Her harsh criticism, manipulations, shaming, and embarrassment are endured by her female body parts. In her young mind, it causes more havoc and more self-doubt. She is burdened by destructive feelings and poisonous, restricting values.

Her daughter gives up after too much violence and acknowledges who she thinks she has become. The narcissistic mother feels liberated and much better about herself. For this moment, her growing up kid is not a threat to her before the next emotional threat occurs. Then, the violence loop will take place all over again.

That form of treatment cannot be recognized by anyone. A young daughter feels frustrated and there could be an uprising. The narcissistic mother fears conflicts and resistance, so she may fail to punish her. It belongs to her, in her mind.

What are we going to do about it? When a teenager is still living with a narcissistic mother, this is a really hard issue.

Many years later, she is able to face the facts and deal with an abusive mother with a demonic history. Saying'NO' to avoid adult violence is never easy. Then, the no-contact decision is life-changing.

It is possible to be free from violence by narcissists. You need the past to be remembered and negative, toxic beliefs and memories discussed. It is possible to disconnect and erase painful memories and emotions from your mind when you do so. Then, vital life force energy will return to your body and easily make you free and resilient.

The narcissistic mother, sadly, never changes. Older, she gets better, mental illness gets stronger, and the individuals she works with are more toxic.

Fixing this individual is never an option as it will never be successful. Remember: a manipulative mother can never be repaired; however, you can save your existence.

Narcissism and their children

Lack of faith drives the sons of narcissistic fathers. Raised by an arrogant, ambitious, self-centered parent, they feel like they will never measure up or be enough to win the approval of their parent. Their father can be absent and manipulating, or critical.

He may belittle and disgrace the errors, weaknesses, weaknesses, or limitations of his son, but brag to his friends about him. He could boast of exaggerated versions of his accomplishments, while disparaging his son's. A narcissistic father, even when the boy is a less-capable child, can ruthlessly bully or compete with his son in games. Likewise, he may be jealous of the attention of his wife to the boy, compete with him, and flirt with his girlfriends or later wife.

Empathy is absent among narcissists. Many fathers of this type are oppressive and strict on how things should be done, the correctness of their beliefs, and how things should be done.

Your utter lack of feeling for the pain and humiliation you might inflict on me with your words and judgments was what was really incomprehensible to me. It was as though you had no knowledge of your strength. I too, I'm sure, sometimes hurt you with what I said, but then I knew it all the time, and it hurt me, but I couldn't contain myself, I couldn't hold back the words, I felt terrible even as I said them. But without much ado, you struck out with your words, you were not sorry for anybody, either during or afterwards, you were absolutely defenseless against yourself.

His father, arrogant and excessively optimistic, listened to no one, but judged everyone without having to be consistent. "The fact that those commandments did not apply to himself made them all the more depressing for Kafka, who outlines the three worlds in which he lived: His laws and decrees were expressed in a" terrible, hoarse undertone of rage and absolute condemnation... [that] only makes me tremble less today than in my childhood...

One in which I, the slave, lived under rules which were invented for me alone and which I could never completely comply with, I didn't know why; then a second world, which was infinitely distant from mine, in which you lived, concerned with government, the issuance of orders and the frustration of not being obeyed; and finally a third world in which everyone else lived peacefully and happily. Either I obeyed your orders, and that was a disgrace, for they applied only to me after all; or

I was defiant, and that was also a disgrace, for how could I presume to defy you; or I could not obey because, for example, I did not have your power, your appetite, your skill, even though you expected it from me as a matter of course; this was the greatest disgrace of all.

Some take over, micro-manage, or are hypercritical when narcissistic fathers get involved with their son's activities. Narcissists are also perfectionists, because nothing is good enough for their child to do-or who he or she is. They become excessively active and influence the lives, education, and dreams of their son, seeing their child as an extension of themselves, as did the father in the movie, "Shine." Alternatively, other fathers may be physically or emotionally distant and wrapped up in their job, addiction, or own pleasures. They behave like it is unimportant and a burden to pay attention to the needs, feelings, and desires of their son or to show up at their games and activities, even though they may provide for him on a material level. These fathers are emotionally unavailable in any situation. They also shame and belittle any sign of distress or weakness in their sons, so they ignore and neglect their own dependence and vulnerability.

Codependence is suffered by children who do not become narcissists themselves. The message they have received is that, despite the fact that they may feel cherished by their mothers, they are somehow insufficient, a burden, and that they do not measure up to their father's standards-ultimately, that they are unworthy of love-because children need to feel that both parents value and love them for who they are. They are profoundly moved to accept, as Kafka explains when he was ill, an apology or crumbs of affection that most people take for granted. When his father merely looked into his room and waved at him, he was overcome with tears. All Kafka wanted was, "a little support, a little friendliness, a little keeping my path open, instead of which you blocked it for me, but with the good intention of making me go another direction, of course." Children of an abusive parent often learn to be self-sufficient, guarded, and devalue their dependence and emotional needs, leading to problems of intimacy. They may marry a cold, critical, or emotionally unavailable narcissist, abuser, anybody.

In an effort to get recognition and their father's approval, sons will be motivated to succeed, but their success sounds hollow. And for themselves, that's never enough. They need to learn to be assertive and to set limits on growing up in safe ways that are not modelled and unimaginable. They must also respect themselves and increase their self-esteem and trust. Due to growing up in a family in perpetual turmoil and/or missing emotional closeness, many have suffered from lifelong inner isolation. However, it is feasible to cure their guilt and to learn to console, embrace, and enjoy themselves and receive love.

Could love be a narcissist?

"They're torn between their love and their pain, between staying and leaving, but they can't seem to do anything. Someone who's loved the narcissistic wonders," Does he really love me?" "Does she accept me? Some swear that they are loved; some are persuaded that they are not. It's confusing, because often the caring person they love, whose business is a joy, is encountered only to be accompanied by actions that makes them feel unimportant or insufficient. Narcissists claim to love their partners and their friends, but do they?

For a narcissist, the challenges

True love is not romance, and co-dependence is not. "For Aristotle and St. Thomas Aquinas, it is" to desire the good of another. "Nathaniel Branden notes in The Psychology of Romantic Love that" To love a human being is to recognize and love his or her person. (1980, p. 50) It is a union of two people that demands that we see another person as distinct from ourselves. Moreover, Erich Fromm (1945) emphasizes in The Art of Loving that love implies performance.

We show active consideration for their lives and development when we love. While it may vary from ours, we strive to consider their perspective and world view. Caring requires giving attention, appreciation, encouragement, compassion, and acceptance. We need to dedicate the time and discipline required. Romantic love may develop into love, but narcissists are not driven to truly know and understand others.

Narcissists lack empathy, according to the Diagnostic and Statistical Manual of Mental Disorders. They are "unwilling to understand or agree with others' emotions and needs." Evidence indicates that they have neurological defects associated with emotional empathy in brain regions. Thus, their ability to respond emotionally adequately and express care

There are several barriers to loving narcissists. First, they perceive neither themselves nor others clearly. First, rather than separate people with various needs, preferences, and emotions, they experience people as extensions of themselves. Second, they overestimate their own emotional empathy. Third, their defenses distort their experiences and relationships with others.

Can we quantify love?

Love is hard to quantify, but research shows that people feel love conveyed by: 1) words of affirmation,

2) spending quality time,

3) giving gifts,

4) acts of service, and

5) physical contact.

Another research revealed that participants have felt loved by a partner who:

1) showed interest in their affairs;

2) gave them emotional and moral support;

(3) revealed intimate facts;

CHAPTER SIX

NARCISSISTIC ABUSE

Narcissists don't love themselves for real. They're actually motivated by guilt. It is the idealized picture of themselves that they admire, that they persuade themselves that they represent. But deep down, the difference between the mask they offer the world and their shame-based selves is felt by narcissists. To stop feeling the guilt, they work hard. This difference is also valid for other codependents, but a narcissist uses methods of defense that are detrimental to relationships and inflict distress and harm to the self-esteem of their loved ones.

Some of the coping mechanisms of the narcissist are violent, hence the word narcissistic violence. "Anyone, however, may be violent, but not a narcissist. Addicts and persons with other mental conditions are also manipulative, as are certain codependents without a mental illness, such as bi-polar disorder and anti-social personality disorder (sociopathy) and borderline personality disorders. Abuse is abuse, regardless of the abuser's diagnosis. The key obstacles for you if you're a victim of violence are:

- Identifying it clearly;
- Construction of a support scheme; and
- Learning how yourself can be improved and secured.

Narcissist Abuse

Mental, physical, financial, spiritual or sexual violence can be abusive. Here are a few instances of violence that you may not have found:

Verbal abuse: Involves belittling, insulting, accusing, blaming, humiliating, requesting, ordering, intimidating, condemning, sarcasm, raging, opposing, undermining, interfering, blocking, and calling for names. Notice that many individuals make demands sometimes, use sarcasm, interrupt, oppose, condemn, blame, or block you. Before labeling it narcissistic misuse, consider the meaning, malice, and frequency of the behavior.

Manipulation: Manipulation is usually an indirect impact on others to act in a way that supports the manipulator's objectives. Often, covert hostility is displayed. Think of a "wolf in sheep's clothing." The words seem innocuous on the surface-even complimentary; yet you feel demeaned or feel a hostile intent underneath. You might not know it as such if you witnessed manipulation growing up.

Emotional blackmail: Threats, frustration, warnings, coercion, or retribution can involve emotional blackmail. It's a form of deception that causes you to have doubt. Sometimes referred to as "FOG," you feel anxiety, responsibility, and or guilt.

Gaslighting: Deliberately making you mistrust or assume that you are psychologically deficient in your views of truth.

Competition: striving and one-upping, often by dishonest means, to always be on top. Examples involve cheating in a game.

Negative contrast: Unnecessarily make similarities with the narcissist or other individuals to contrast you negatively.

Sabotage: For the intent of vengeance or personal gain, destructive interference with your endeavors or relationships.

Exploitation and objectification: Without regard to your feelings or needs, exploiting or taking advantage of you for personal ends.

Lying: persistent deceit in order to escape transparency or to reach the own ends of the narcissist.

Withholding: Withholding from you items such as money, gender, contact or affection.

Neglect: Ignoring the needs of a child who is accountable to the abuser. This involves child harm, i.e. putting or leaving a child in a dangerous situation.

Invasion of privacy: by going through your things, phone, mail, ignoring your boundaries; refusing your physical privacy or stalking or trailing you; ignoring the privacy you have asked for.

Assassination or defamation of character: Transmitting to other people false rumors or lies about you.

Violence: This involves blocking your movement, hair pulling, throwing stuff, or damaging your house.

Financial abuse: Financial abuse can involve manipulating you by economic domination or through extortion, fraud, manipulation, or gambling, or by accruing debt on your behalf or selling your personal property, draining your finances.

Isolation: Isolating you by control, manipulation, verbal violence, character assassination, or other means of violence, from friends, relatives, or access to outside resources and support.

On a scale, narcissism and the severity of violence occur. It can range from suppressing your emotions to physical abuse. Narcissists usually do not take responsibility for their actions and pass the blame to you or others; however, some do and are capable of experiencing remorse and self-reflection.

Sociopathy and Malignant Narcissism

"One who acts in a malicious, violent way with more narcissistic features is known to have" malignant narcissism. "Malignant narcissists are not troubled by remorse. They can be sadistic and enjoy causing pain. They can be so competitive and unprincipled that anti-social behaviour is involved. Paranoia as a form of self-protection places them in a defensive-attack mode.

Malignant narcissism may be similar to sociopathy. Sociopaths have brains which are malformed or impaired. They exhibit signs of narcissism, but not all narcissists are sociopathic. Their motives vary. In order to fulfill their self-serving agenda, while narcissists prop up an ideal identity to be respected, sociopaths alter who they

95

are. At all costs, they need to succeed and think little about violating social standards and rules. As narcissists do, they do not bind to individuals. They don't want to be abandoned by narcissists. They rely on the acceptance of others, but sociopaths can easily walk away from interactions that do not benefit them. Although some narcissists often scheme to accomplish their aims, they are typically more reactive than sociopaths, who measure their plans coldly.

Abusers of Narcissists

However, as most people think about abuse-be it spousal, maternal, etc.-they prefer to concentrate on physical abuse, the residual effects of any abuse may be catastrophic. Mental and emotional abuse can be just as harmful, especially when the abuser is someone close to the abused individual.

Perhaps the worst kind of violence comes from the hands of those who are so worried with themselves that they do not see or think about the consequences of their actions. In several distinct types of relationships, including parent-child, spouse / significant others, and even friendships, this form of narcissistic violence can be found. Emotional abuse by a narcissistic parent may be particularly insidious since it may damage the capacity of the child in the future to develop healthy relationships. It has been suggested that those who have experienced emotional abuse as children appear to end up in similar abusive relationships as adults due to a lack of an acceptable model of a healthy relationship.

The 1980s in the United States were seen as a time when it was predicted that self-centeredness and egocentrism were not only appropriate. Fresh extremes of narcissism were generated by the "Me Generation." For their own sake, many were able to ignore others' well-being.

Despite this inner emphasis, in the strictest sense, most of the people we think of when we think of this moment in time were not true narcissists. The word narcissism comes from the Greek tale of Naissus, a hunter who was the son of Cephissus, the river god, and Liriope, the nymph. He possessed such elegance that he was not even free of the lure himself. The god Nemesis fooled him into staring into a pool, whereupon he saw and fell in love with his own reflection, only to die considering his own fair features there.

In psychoanalytic terms, narcissism is characterized as "excessive obsession with oneself; excessive self-love; vanity" or as "erotic pleasure derived from the appreciation of one's own physical or mental qualities, being a natural condition at the infantile level of personality growth." In 1968, as a definitive diagnosis, a severe type was introduced to the psychiatric literature.

The American Psychiatric Association's latest Diagnostic and Statistical Manual (DSM- V) describes Narcissistic Personality Disorder as:

In fantasy or actions, a persistent pattern of grandiosity, need for respect and lack of empathy, starting from early adulthood and present in a variety of contexts, as five (or more) of the following indicate:

1. Has a grandiose sense of self-importance (e.g., exaggerates accomplishments and abilities, expects without commensurate accomplishments to be regarded as superior).

2. Fantasies of infinite prosperity, strength, brilliance, elegance, or ideal love are involved.

3. It assumes that he or she is "important" and unique and can only be understood by other

important or high-status individuals (or institutions) or should be identified with them.

4. Excessive admiration is required.

5. Has a sense of entitlement, i.e. unrealistic expectations, or automatic compliance with his or her expectations, of particularly favorable treatment.

6. It is interpersonally exploitative, i.e., to accomplish its own ends, it takes advantage of others.

7. Lacks empathy: is unable to consider others' emotions and needs or to identify with them.

8. He or she is also envious of others or assumes that others envy him or her.

9. Demonstrates rude, haughty attitudes or actions.

Furthermore, to support a diagnosis of Narcissistic Personality Disorder, the following conditions must be met:

A.

Significant impairments in the functioning of personality occur through:

1. Self-Functioning Impairments (a or b):

a. Identity: excessive self-definition and self-esteem management comparison to others; exaggerated self-assessment can be inflated or deflated, or vacillate between extremes; emotional regulation mirrors self-esteem fluctuations.

b. Self-direction: Goal-setting is focused on other people's approval; personal expectations are unreasonably high in order to see oneself as exceptional, or too low focused on a sense of entitlement; sometimes ignorant of one's own motives.

AND

2. Interpersonal functioning impairments (a or b):

a. Empathy: diminished capacity to accept or identify with the

Emotions and desires of others; overly attuned to other people's reactions, but only if viewed as important to oneself; over-estimating or underestimating one's own effects on others.

b. Intimacy: Relationships are mostly shallow and exist to control self-esteem; mutuality is limited by little real interest in other interactions and the desire for personal benefit predominates.

In the following domain, pathological personality traits:

1. Antagonism, distinguished by:

a. Grandiosity: entitlement emotions, either overt or covert;

Self-centeredness; strongly clinging to the idea that one is greater than others; against others, condescending.

b. Attention seeking: excessive attempts to attract and be the object of other people's attention; seeking admiration.

c. The impairments in the functioning of personality and the presentation of personality traits of the individual are relatively constant over time and consistent through circumstances.

d. The impairments in personality functioning and the personality trait presentation of the individual are not best understood as normative for the developmental process or socio-cultural context of the individual.

e. The personality functioning impairments and the personality trait manifestation of the individual are not exclusively attributable to the direct physiological effects of a drug (e.g., abuse drug, medication) or a general medical condition (e.g., serious head trauma).

Although all of this can sound daunting, we can see how a relationship with someone with Narcissistic Personality Disorder might quickly become a living Nightmare by concentrating on a few key portions of the diagnosis. As mentioned in the first quote, people with Narcissistic Personality Disorder have been found to be more valuable than other individuals. They not only put themselves on a pedestal, but they also believe that others do the same. A healthy relationship is not one in which one person lords over the other, but healthy relationships cannot be formed by these narcissists.

There is an inability to form proper attachments due to a lack of empathy for others or to form interpersonal relationships, as we see in the second quote. The fact that "Relationships [are] mostly superficial and exist to serve the regulation of self-esteem" is particularly telling (emphasis added).

A link is a one-way street with someone with Narcissistic Personality Disorder. All of the emotional support and attention flows from the person to the narcissist. Verbal and emotional abuse, belittling, moaning, and even physical abuse characterize these relationships. Narcissists feel that they can do no wrong, so the fault of the other person is any issues with the relationship- and even issues that occur in everyday life. The partner is somehow the one to blame if a mistake is made.

The need for recognition and admiration from narcissists causes them to actively seek out others who can validate their inflated sense of self-worth. This leads to a variety of short encounters and a long line of discarded partners. There is a high possibility that he or she would not be loyal if the narcissist is married. Naturally, the partner would be responsible for not being pretty enough, loving enough, etc., if infidelity is detected.

Similar traits are also presented by victims of a narcissistic abuser. A low sense of self-worth, often followed by an inability to make choices for themselves, is the most popular. They spend years being told that they are not good enough, that they are not smart enough, that they are not good enough. They have come to internalize these derogatory comments over time. They question their own expertise. This makes them more dependent on the narcissistic abuser, causing a co-dependency loop.

In terms of parental treatment, this is one of the most alarming aspects of narcissistic abuse. They grow up thinking that they are not worthy because kids are continually belittled. When they are actually beyond their abusive parent's influence, they lack the coping skills needed to live on their own. They gravitate toward someone who can tolerate them despite their self-perceived shortcomings and make choices for them, doubting their own decision-making skills and crippled by low self-esteem. In short, with narcissistic abusers, they enter into relationships. They just abandon their parents to end up with someone just like the same people who in the first place exploited them.

Many that have suffered at the hands of a narcissist may exhibit any number of emotional and physical signs that may be hard to attribute to the relationship as they are a result of the stress they experience on a daily basis. Confusion, disassociation, bad eating and sleeping habits, and even Post Traumatic Stress Disorder (PTSD) symptoms are among these.

It is extremely difficult for someone in a relationship with a narcissist to seek support as they have been conditioned for most if not all decision-making processes to look at their abuser. Their low sense of self-worth makes it possible for the belief that they deserve better to be overlooked. In their eyes, clearly, no one else will have them. Despite the fact that they are unhappy, they should be content with the relationship they have. This is a theme that the offender would also perpetuate.

It is possible to break the cycle of narcissistic violence, but it is difficult. The first step must be to acknowledge that no one is worthy of the narcissist's relentless degradation and demands.

As the self-image is restored to a healthier level, without the abuser's input, it becomes simpler to make decisions. Of course, this is an incredibly complex process that could require the assistance of outsiders, including professionals. Sadly, it is common for narcissistic abusers to limit the access of their partners to others, especially those who may express views contrary to their grandiose sense of self.

CHAPTER SEVEN

THE NARCISSISTIC

EMOTIONAL ABUSER ERA

All stuff has their respective seasons. There was a season in your life before the narcissistic emotional abuser. In your life, there was or is a season of the narcissistic emotional abuser. And the season after the narcissistic emotional abuser in your life, certainly, is or may be. As is the normal cycle of life, one season prepares the soil for the next season.

You don't have the issue, "How did I get into this mess on earth?" until the narcissistic emotional abuser invaded your existence. No, most likely years before that issue, you were probably asking yourself the issue, something to the effect of, "Why did he / she / they do this to me?" The question was not about the trauma caused by the narcissistic sexual abuser you fell in love with as an adult. No, that question may have been about the violence caused in your life by a different form of abuser when you were just a girl, many times a sexual abuser.

This is not to suggest that the sexual abuser was not also a narcissist, as sexual offenders show three of the minimum five "diagnosable" requirements required. This is not to suggest that all those who find themselves with stories to share of being associated with a narcissistic emotional abuser were victims of the trauma caused by sexual abuse in childhood. There, however, is the very strong probability that in the early years of your life, someone did something to you that primed your "soil" to attract and be drawn to a narcissistic emotional abuser.

You begin to understand that a transition has started to take place in the way you think and the way you talk, in the midst of being in the season of the narcissistic emotional abuser. At the beginning of this season, your discussions centered on what they, the narcissistic emotional abuser, did or more frequently did not do while talking to others by your side who feel similar to the same emotional distress that you yourself experience due to your repeated return to the abuser. Now, your attention is on asking yourself, "How did I get into this mad mess?" You are starting to remember your success and who you are or what you have achieved in life. In what you want to believe is an intimate relationship, you start comparing yourself to the ones that you know exist.

You begin to do some soul searching in the middle of this season. Your question, "How did I get into this mess?" is not just a glib question anymore. This issue starts miraculously to take on a whole new energy. They want an answer. It demands a response. You are the question's owner and hold the key to give you the answer.

Dealing with The Abuser

How do you treat your abuser?

It seems bleak sometimes. Abusers are cruel, unethical, sadistic, calculated, cunning, persuasive, deceitful-they seem invincible in short. They sway the system in their favor quickly.

Here is a list of countermeasures which are escalating. They reflect the perspective of thousands of victims of violence having been distilled. They will help you to cope with and overcome violence.

Judicial or medical measures are not included. Where applicable, consult an attorney, an accountant, a therapist, or a psychiatrist.

You must decide first:

Would you like to stay with him — or cancel the relationship?

1. I would like to stay with him.

FIVE DON'T DO'S-How to Escape the Narcissist's Wrath

Never argue with or refute the narcissist;

Never give affection to him at all;

Look amazed at whatever attribute matters to him (for example: his professional accomplishments or his good looks, or his popularity with women, etc.);

Never remind him of life out there and link it to his sense of grandiosity if you do, somehow;

Do not make any statements that could impact his self-image, omnipotence, judgment, omniscience, skill, capabilities, professional record, or even omnipresence directly or indirectly.

TEN DO'S-How to make your narcissist dependent on you if you want to stay with him.

Listen to what the narcissist says attentively and agree with it all. Don't believe a word of it, but let it slip as if it were all just right, as normal, business.

Personally, offer the narcissist something completely special that they cannot acquire somewhere else. Be prepared to set up potential primary narcissistic supply outlets for your narcissist as well, since, if at all, you may not be IT for very long. If you take over the narcissist's procuring role, they become so much more dependent on you.

Be patient and go out of your way to be welcoming constantly, thereby keeping the narcissistic supply flowing freely and preserving harmony.

Be unendingly giving. This one may not be appealing to you, but it is a proposal to take it or leave it.

Be completely independent of the narcissist, mentally and financially. Take what you need: enthusiasm and swallowing, and when the narcissist does or does something stupid, disrespectful, or insensitive, he refuses to get angry or hurt. Yelling back works very well, but when you feel your narcissist might be on the verge of leaving you, it should be reserved for special occasions; silent treatment is best as an ordinary reaction, but it must be done without any emotional substance, more with the air of boredom and "I'll speak to you later, when I'm good and ready, and when you're acting more fairly." As you would an infant, handle your narcissist.

Then grant yourself enough permission to have "secret" sex with other people if your narcissist is cerebral and not interested in having a lot of sex. Your cerebral narcissist would not be oblivious to infidelity, so it is paramount to have discretion and privacy.

If your narcissist is somatic and you don't mind, engage in group sex meetings, but make sure you choose your narcissist properly. Leave him, if you do mind. Sex addicts and incurably unfaithful are somatic narcissists.

If you are a "fixer" then, preferably until they become "situations," concentrate on fixing situations. Don't delude yourself for a moment that you can cure the narcissist-it just won't happen.

If there is some remedy that can be found, it is to help the narcissist become aware of their illness, with no detrimental effects or allegations at all in the process. It's like living with a person with a physical disability and being able to negotiate, calmly, unemotionally, what the handicap's disadvantages and advantages are and how the two of you should function with these variables instead of attempting to change them.

Last but not least, and most important of all: know yourself.

What do you get from this relationship? Are you a masochist actually? Codependent? Codependent? Why is this relationship fascinating and appealing?

Define for yourself what positive and advantageous things in this relationship you think you are getting.

Define the aspects you find detrimental to you. To mitigate the risk to yourself, build techniques.

Don't expect that the narcissist would be able to negotiate with you cognitively to alter who they are. In getting your narcissist to tone down on the very negative habits that influence you, you can have some modest success-but this can only be done in a really trusting, honest and open relationship.

(1a) Focus on Your Boundaries-Stop Harassment

Refuse manipulative conduct to embrace it. Request actions and responses that are fairly predictable and reasonable. Insist on upholding the constraints, interests, preferences, and goals you have.

Request the treatment be equal and proportional. Reject or neglect conduct that is unfair and capricious.

Reacting in kind, if you are up to the inevitable confrontation. Let him taste some medicine of his own.

Never show the abuser that he is scared of you. Do not use bullies to bargain. They're so insatiable. To blackmail, do not succumb.

If things get rough — disengage, involve or (legally) threaten law enforcement officers, friends and colleagues.

Don't hold a key to your abuse. Secrecy is the weapon of the abuser.

Never give him a second opportunity. Respond to the first transgression with your full arsenal.

Be under guard. In a first or informal meeting, don't be too forthcoming. Collect intelligence.

Only be yourself. Do not distort your expectations, limits, priorities, goals, and red lines.

Do not act incoherently. On your word, don't go back. Be firm and definitive.

Keep away from quagmires like these. No matter how innocuous, scrutinize every bid and suggestion.

Prepare arrangements for backups. Keep others aware of your whereabouts and your condition as assessed.

Be watchful and doubtful. Don't make yourself gullible and suggestible. Secure better than sorry.

The abuser's proxies are often unaware of their position. Just expose him. Notify them. Show them how the abuser abuses them, misuses them, and makes easy use of them.

Trap the abuser of yours. As he treats you, treat him. Get others involved. Take it into the open. Nothing to disinfect the violence, like sunshine.

(1b) Mimic His Actions

Mirror the actions of the narcissist and echo his terms.

If, for example, he has an anger attack-rage back. If threatened-threaten back and attempt to use the same language and material credibly. When he leaves the home, he leaves the house and dies. Act suspicious if he is suspicious. Go down to his stage, be critical, denigrating, humiliating.

(1c) Terrify Him

Identify the narcissist's vulnerabilities and susceptibilities and strike repeated, escalating blows at them.

Use the knowledge of it to intimidate him if a narcissist has a secret or something he wants to hide. Drop vague clues that the incidents and newly discovered evidence are enigmatic witnesses. Do it in an escalating way, cleverly, non-committally, progressively.

Let the rest be done by his imagination. Except for uttering a vague reference, making an ominous allusion, delineating a potential turn of events, you don't have to do anything.

It is important to add that all these operations must be lawfully pursued, ideally through the good services of law offices and in broad daylight. They could constitute extorting or extortion, abuse and a host of other criminal offenses if handled in the wrong way.

(1d) Attract Him

Give him Narcissistic Supply continued. By offering, withholding, or threatening to withhold narcissistic supplies (adulation, appreciation, affection, sex, awe, subservience, etc.), you can make a narcissist do something.

(1e) Playing on his Fear of Abandonment

If nothing else works, they threaten to abandon him directly.

The threat may be conditional ("If you don't do anything, or if you do it, I'm going to leave you").

Even if they are not intended as such, narcissists view the following as threats of abandonment:

Confrontation, simple conflict, and lengthy criticism

When entirely neglected

When you demand that your boundaries, desires, feelings, choices, preferences are respected,

As you retaliate (scream back at him, for example).

II. I can't bear it any longer — I wanted to leave him

(iia) In Court, Battle Him

Here are a few of the devastating things the narcissist discovers, particularly in a court of law, such as during a deposition:

Any argument or evidence that seems to contradict his inflated image of his grandiose self. Any criticism, disagreement, disclosure of false successes, belittling of "talents and abilities" that the narcissist fantasizes he has, any suggestion that he is subordinate, subjugated, dominated, owned or dependent on a third party. Any classification, indistinguishable from many others, of the narcissist as average and popular. Any sign that the narcissist is poor, needy, dependent, defective, sluggish, not intelligent, naive, gullible, prone, not knowledgeable, tampered with, a victim.

The narcissist is likely to react to all of these with anger and he is likely to reveal evidence and stratagems he had no conscious intention of revealing in an attempt to re-establish his fantastic grandiosity.

The narcissist responds to a violation of what he perceives as his right with narcissistic anger, hate, hostility, or abuse. The narcissist would be inflamed by every insinuation, hint, intimation, or overt declaration that the narcissist is not at all unique, that he is ordinary, normal, not even sufficiently idiosyncratic to merit a fleeting interest.

Tell the narcissist that he does not deserve the best treatment, that his needs are not the priority of anyone, that he is dull, that an ordinary professional (doctor, accountant, lawyer, psychiatrist) can tend to his needs, that he and his motivations are clear and can be easily assessed, that he will do what he is told, that his temper tantrums will not be tolerated, that no particular tantrums will be tolerated,

"The narcissist is contradicted, exposed, insulted, and berated" (You're not as intelligent as you think you are," "Who's really behind all this? It takes sophistication that you don't seem to have," "So, you don't have formal schooling," "you're (mistake his age, make him far older) ... I'm sorry, you're... Young" "What have you been doing with your life? Have you studied? Have you got a degree? Have you ever formed or managed a company? Would you describe yourself as an achievement? "Will your children share your opinion that you are a good father?", "The last time you were seen was with Ms...." She is a cleaning lady (suppressed grin) (in demeaning disbelief).'

Be equipped with completely unambiguous, first class, fully authenticated and vouched for data.

(IIb) If you have common children
In "The Guilt of the Abused-Pathologizing the Victim" I explained how the mechanism against the victim is biased and named.

Regrettably, professionals and practitioners of mental health-marital and couple therapists, psychologists-are conditioned to respond favorably to particular verbal signals through years of indoctrinating and dogmatic schooling.

The paradigm is that violence is seldom one-sided- in other words, it is invariably "triggered" either by the victim or by the abuser's mental health issues. Another common lie is that one way (talk therapy) or another (medication) will effectively cure all mental health problems.

This transfers the blame from the attacker to his prey. The abused may have done something to bring on their own violence or have actually been "inaccessible" mentally to assist the abuser with his issues. Recovery is guaranteed if only the victim is able to engage and connect with the abuser in a treatment plan. So goes the orthodoxy.

The therapist is unfairly judged by refusal to do so- in other words, refusal to risk more violence. The victim is branded uncooperative, stubborn, or even abusive!

Therefore, the key is feigned acquiescence and collaboration with the method of the therapist, acknowledgement of his / her understanding of the events, and the use of key phrases such as: "I want to communicate / work with (the abuser)", "trauma", "relationship", "healing process", "inner child", "children's fine", "fathering value", "significant others" and other psycho-babble.

Above all, do not be assertive or offensive and do not criticise or argue directly with the therapist.

I make the therapist sound like another possible abuser because he / she becomes one in several situations when they collude with the abuser unwittingly, invalidate the perceptions of abuse, and pathologize the victim.

(IIc) Refuse all interactions

Be sure to retain as much interaction with your abuser as required by the courts, advisers, mediators, guardians, or law enforcement officers.

Do NOT contravene the system's decisions. Operate from the inside to alter judgments, assessments, or rulings, but NEVER rebel or defy them. You're just going to turn the system against you and your interests.

But refuse any and all gratuitous interaction with the narcissist, with the exception of the minimum required by the courts.

Do not respond to his e-mails that are begging, sentimental, nostalgic, flattering, or intimidating.

Get all the presents he's giving you back.

Refuse him to access your premises. Do not respond to the intercom, either.

Do not speak on the phone with him. Hang up the moment you hear his voice while making it clear to him, in a single sentence, respectful but firm, that you are determined not to speak to him.

Do not answer letters from him.

On special occasions, or in emergencies, do not visit him.

Do not respond to questions, demands or pleas transmitted by third parties to you.

Disconnect from third parties which, at his request, you know are spying on you.

Do not speak with your children about him.

Don't babble about him.

Even if you are in desperate need, do not ask him for anything.

Do not discuss your personal life-or his-when you are forced to face him.

Relegate, when and where possible, any unavoidable interaction with him to professionals: your counsel, or your accountant.

CHAPTER EIGHT

SIGNS TO NOTE THAT YOU'RE WITH A NARCISSIST

Everyone writes about narcissists in such great detail, and goes to great lengths to justify their conduct, but no one ever speaks about their enablers; those who facilitate the abusers, those behind them who help them unconsciously and allow them to continue.

There are their other half, so to speak, and, at least for their incompetence, are just as accountable as the narcissist. They don't want to be exploited by them knowingly, but they support it and do nothing about it to defend themselves or others.

And no other form of enabler is more facilitating and central to violence, and can do more than victims of narcissists to avoid it by resisting it. This is because, in getting their needs met right now, narcissists are so demanding, high-maintenance and ruthless. They rely so heavily on their enablers to work and their encouragement. Or, even more precisely, those who harass the perpetrators and take the brunt of the harass.

I'm willing to be sure more individuals fall into this category than the former, and if we were to concentrate and deal with this issue adequately for assertively, there will be far less individuals putting up with, perpetuating and allowing narcissistic conduct to proceed.

Abuse damages the abusers and the enablers, but the enablers do the same. I'm willing to bet that it causes more harm than violence simply because it allows the violence to occur and promotes it, thereby causing more abuse in the world. It is a source of inspiration.

You must be an enabler if you meet or are in some way voluntarily involved with a narcissist. If you are, let's find out.

1. You are supposed to over-accommodate and compromise for them, then get nothing back and are never valued for it.

You put the needs of others, at your expense, above your own. By putting the narcissist's desires above theirs, you have harmed the people who really need you.

Another way of saying this is that while you are still accommodating someone else, you do nothing for yourself. You're too busy meeting the needs of someone else (read it, demands) to meet your own or even take care of someone who, like children, depends solely on you.

It also means that to neglect your own, or to even disregard your own detriments in the name of another, you are concerned with the affairs of others. In your capacity to accept and then recognize your real issues, such as violence, you feel powerless, far less fix them yourself.

Persistently, eternally and ruthlessly, the narcissists resist. They're going to do whatever they can to make sure you can't interrupt what they do, because they don't have to change. The whole thing is just running away. It's a sprint, and at every turn they have to keep ahead of you. That's what they care about.

They just run away, run away far and wide, in all the ways they can, to somewhere else, because they just can't take it. What do we know? We don't know what they're feeling. But I know for sure that hanging around and feeling the pain, and spreading it around, magnifying and worsening through your capacity, is not our work.

Another indication is that, no matter how much it costs you directly or comes at your expense, you are over-accommodating and giving in to their demands.

By doing as they ask, when they ask and continue to put up with them, and persuade yourself as much, you can tell yourself you are being a good person.

You'll reassure yourself that they mean well when they get violent, but do not know how to express themselves carefully. In other words, because that's what you need to believe to justify having to do something about it, you'll put the violence in endearing terms. Truth be told, and you already know this so that you can guess what I'm about to tell you, is that by promoting their fantasy and running yourself ragged and spreading yourself thin, you are actually assisting them.

In the rape, you're their accomplice and complicit. Don't get me wrong now, you don't sound like that. They make you believe that by sacrificing yourself and putting their interests above your own, you are a hero for putting up with them and making things right, doing everything you have to do to help and protect others.

In fact, what you really do is endorse a toxic cycle and a regressive pattern of behavior that all depends on whatever mood they happen to be in.

They make you a chump because you fail to understand that their issues and problems are just ruses to bring you into a place of misery and agony, so that when they sit on their throne, wait and whine when you do a bad job, you can scramble to fix it.

They tell you that they are right for you, and that's why you're staying. But they're just not doing any good at all, because they're just trying to hurt you because keep doing it, like a parasite, until you die and they have to find someone else. That sounds very dramatic, but it's true; they set themselves up for life by getting their problems burdened by someone else.

Since we can't stop being judged and everyone seems to have an opinion about you that these days they just have to share with somebody else, you're bound to come across what someone else thinks about you and not like it.

The enabler is crippled with fear of being punished by others and tries to correct their error and apologize to the person even though they are really the ones in the right, which is possibly because enablers do very little, only incompetence and convenient denial, in the way of purposely harming other people.

You will be too concentrated and concerned with the needs of others, especially when they are artificial and designed to get your attention away from something and funnel it on them; coercion and dependency, helplessness learned.

How can you say if they're sure they're doing that? It's the same thing at all times, and it never changes, because they never change.

They never better themselves, and so their problems never better. In the same place, at the same time and in the same mentality, they're still trapped. Since they are not working, they're unstable, you cannot find working ways of treating them.

Codependence

You both support and complement the dysfunctional behavior of each other through your own dysfunctional behavior.

Dependence runs the whole gambit from having to be in constant contact with each other to having to take over and make choices for each other, from being unable to do it yourself to wanting their permission to do anything, and their acceptance that you did it "right" (which you never will). It goes in both directions.

Now that the last part may seem unusual, isn't one entity dependent and the other independent? One is more independent than the other, yeah, and that is you. You're not the one who makes an illusion and you're not the one who wants to manipulate it all.

Exactly what is control? What is influence and power over the life of someone else? It's an illusion to run and govern your life, and the object of that illusion is to deny their reliance on you. They're with you because they're necessary for you, not the other way around. But all of this is a ruse to hide their own reliance on you and project their concerns on you.

It seems odd now that they don't appear to be or behave like you're being pushed into a situation, don't they? Technically speaking, they're not pushing you to, right? Technically, yes, but not for practical purposes.

You would also accept it as a power if you understood what they were doing and observed it for what it really is, what they're thinking and how they regard it. Bear in mind that this is also still acknowledged to them. They know what's right and good, or they're not going to be so good at being bad. They either don't care, or worse, they enjoy being evil, malevolent, harming others.

In other words, they do not "CONTROL!!!" by steering, guiding and directing your actions, and especially by obstructing you, because it weakens you, they "control" your favorite things to do. But mainly, they will calculate their actions so that they make a clear decision that they want from you, expected and intended reaction.

Dependence also comes with denial, rationalizations and explanations for how dependent you really are. You're going to come up with these, naturally, to convince yourself you're in a good spot.

Negative relationships

Through hate and confrontation, and as a result, you feel bad and don't know why you relate to others

This one is difficult to spot without input from others.

You polarize yourself from other people when you find yourself drawing big lines between you and other people you like for trivial reasons, and become a less desirable person yourself.

It is a high priority of the narcissist to lose contact with family and friends, to become the only source of feedback, the bridge to reality, or their reality, which is not very much like reality at all.

With narcissists, it's all worked out for you already: it's poor. Black and white thought, negative prejudice, detrimental interactions with others and the outside world, which you would often feel alienated, distanced and separated from more and more.

You're scared of success and of earning what you deserve. Your empowerment means that they lose control of you, personal or financial success, and then this means that they praise you for being idle and not doing anything at all, which makes them feel the most relaxed, protected and in control of you. They can't regulate themselves, so by manipulating you, they compensate and make up for it.

No real actionable measures are taken or progress towards their specified objectives is made. Nothing really happens, nothing changes at all. There's a lot of conversation going on about doing stuff, but nothing really comes out of it. That's because just as it is right now, they want it.

They're just drawing you and themselves to the promise of change, but they're too afraid to change, and they just don't want to. They like the everlasting bond between parent and child that you two have, which takes me to the next sign: it changes all the time between who is the parent and who is the child. They usually want to be the authoritative figure you are responding to, but they need you to tell them what to do when they're afraid, or else they can't work. Dependency is that.

You will feel terrible, but you will not know why exactly. With almost 90 percent accuracy, I would basically guarantee that you're with a narcissist if this is the case. There are simply no other personality disorders that, without you noticing, can do this, otherwise you will know and notice it, or at least believe it.

Let me ask you something: Have they ever supported you or supported you openly? What do they talk to other people about you? Positive, is it? What do they like about you and what do they admire? What would you mean, and then what would they mean are your greatest abilities? Do you know, for sure, their answer to any of these questions?

That's because you're never going to know, they're not going to tell you and they're not going to respect you. They're not really fond of you. They project onto you every enemy they've ever had, someone who's ever done wrong to them because they couldn't resolve what that person did to them, so they hate, and they hate and they smoke, and they vent their socially "legitimate" ways, even though they're not at all and utterly inappropriate, but you're still putting up with them.

They don't like you, and it's a safe bet that because you're putting up with it right now, you're used to anyone disliking you, so this definitely isn't your first, second, or even last time being in this situation.

If you believe there's something wrong, there probably is. That narcissists make your emotions taboo and persuade you that you should not listen to them is the reason why it becomes strange and feels bad to suspect.

For narcissists, making you feel unsure of yourself is their greatest priority, and making you believe it's all an accident.

They measure their actions against your own personality to see what effect it has on you, to optimize every effort and make every effort to harm, manipulate, and break you down. It's no mistake, it's on purpose.

CHAPTER NINE

NARCISSISTS AND WHY THEY ACT THE WAY THEY DO

With their charming side, you will fall in love and be devastated by their dark side. It can be baffling, but when you realize what drives them, it all makes sense. You are shielded from their games, lies, and exploitation by that knowledge.

There is an impaired or undeveloped self in narcissists. They think and act differently from other individuals. Because of the way their brain is wired, whether due to nature or nurture, they behave as they do. The seriousness of narcissism varies. Some individuals, with greater severity, have more symptoms, whereas other narcissists have less, milder symptoms. Thus, the following discussion does not apply to the same degree to all narcissists.

Vulnerability of Narcissists

Narcissists are actually very weak despite possessing seemingly powerful personalities. They are considered by psychotherapists to be "fragile." They suffer from extreme loneliness, emptiness, powerlessness, and loss of sense. They crave power because of their intense weakness and must vigilantly monitor their environment, the people around them, and their feelings. Intolerable signs of vulnerability in themselves and in others are shows of fragile emotions, such as anxiety, guilt, or sorrow. Their below-discussed protection mechanism protects them, but harms other citizens. They're more malicious when they feel most vulnerable and the result of their acts is meaningless.

Narcissistic embarrassment

There is toxic guilt under their façade, which could be subconscious. Shame causes narcissists to feel vulnerable and insufficient feelings of insecurity that they have to deny to themselves and others. This is one reason why, even when supposed to be positive, they do not handle criticism, accountability, opposition, or negative feedback.

Rather, they seek unconditional, constructive consideration from others.

Arrogant spirit

They cultivate an attitude of superiority to compensate for feeling inferior. Some people, including whole groups they deem inferior, such as refugees, a ethnic minority, a lower economic class, or people with less education, are often rude, critical, and disdainful of them. They bring down others, like bullies, to pick themselves up.

Terrifying factor

Their disguised embarrassment accounts for their self-aggrandizement and braggadocio. They strive to persuade themselves and others to succeed, to be uniquely exceptional and to be the best, the brightest, the wealthiest, the most beautiful, the most talented. This is also why narcissists gravitate towards individuals, colleges, organisations, and other entities of celebrity and high status. Being among the best convinces them that they're better than most, though they aren't so sure internally.

Entitlement mentality

Whatever their actions, narcissists feel entitled to get what they want from others. Their sense of superiority hides their guilt and vulnerability from inside. They are persuaded they are superior and it follows that they deserve special treatment. They have a more precious time than most, for instance, and they shouldn't have to wait in line like the masses. What they might expect from others is not limited. Interpersonal relationships are a one-way path, so other persons (see below) are considered inferior and not distinct from them. Their conduct is not known as hypocritical, since they feel superior and unique. For other citizens, laws don't apply to them.

Lack of Humanity

The capacity of narcissists to respond emotionally and convey suitable care and concern is significantly impaired. Narcissists lack empathy, as per the Diagnostic and Statistical Manual of Mental Disorders. They are "unwilling to understand or interact with others' emotions and needs. Research indicates that in brain regions associated with social empathy, they have anatomical defects."

They may say they love you, but you have to decide if you feel loved by the way they treat you. Real love needs empathy, consideration, and deep comprehension of the individual we care about. We display active concern for the life and development of that individual. While it may vary from ours, we strive to understand their perspective and world view. If you have not experienced such true love, or it has been mixed with violence

Narcissists may be greedy, hurtful, and cold without empathy when it does not help them to be charming or cooperative. Relationships are transactional to them. They are interested in getting their needs meta-sometimes rather than reacting to emotions, even if it means manipulating others, stealing, lying, or breaking the law. Although in the early stages of a r r they can feel enthusiasm and passion

Voidness

Narcissists lack a meaningful, emotional link to themselves, making it impossible for them to communicate with others emotionally. Their undeveloped self and lack of internal resources force them to rely on others for affirmation. They are simply afraid that they are unacceptable rather than confidence. They can only admire themselves in others' eyes as mirrored. Thus, despite their boasts

Lack of Limits

Mythological Narcissus, as reflected in a pool of water, fell in love with his own portrait. He did not know at first that it was himself. This defines narcissists metaphorically. The inner emptiness, guilt, and undeveloped selves of narcissists render them unsure of their boundaries. They do not experience other people as distinct entities, but as two-dimensional extensions of themselves, without confidence

Defenses of Narcissists

It's the defensive mechanisms that narcissists use to defend their insecurity that make relationships with narcissists so challenging. Arrogance and disdain, denial, projection, hostility, and jealousy are typical defenses they use.

Arrogance and disrespect

These defenses inflate the ego of a narcissist with an aura of superiority to defend against latent feelings of inadequacy. By imposing inferiority on others, it often transfers guilt.

Denial Factor

Denial distorts reality so that a narcissist can live to defend their fragile ego in an inflated bubble of their own fantasy universe. They misrepresent, rationalize, manipulate truth, and delude themselves to prevent something that can trigger a chink in their armour, which is so thick that no amount of proof or argument can get through to some narcissists.

Forecast and fault

This protection enables someone else to be disowned and psychologically or verbally linked to inappropriate emotions, perceptions or attributes. Blame changes guilt, because the narcissist is blameless. This protection plays the same function as denial. Projecting is an implicit mechanism, whereby a narcissist may not have to encounter something unpleasant in him or herself, but sees everything as external.

Aggression Behavior

Through driving people away, violence is used to establish defense. Narcissists perceive the environment as violent and dangerous, and both in word and action, they move violently towards people. This may lead to harassment of narcissism. Vindictive narcissists retaliate to reverse feelings of shame and regain their dignity through destroying their abuser.

Envy

The best would be narcissists. They can't take joy in the success of anyone else. If anyone else has what they want, it makes them feel inferior. Life is a game of zero-sum. Not only do competitive narcissists envy people who have what they want; they will respond vengefully to bring them down, particularly if they feel threatened. With their children, narcissists are also envious and competitive.

It's really beneficial to realize who you're dealing with, but it's more important to figure out what you can do. If you love a narcissist, the Dealing with a Narcissist exercises and techniques can be beneficial and offer you clarity about how to satisfy your needs and how to decide whether to remain in the relationship.

The response to your "How" may well come from your "Why" response.

If you have had the unpleasant experience of crossing paths with a narcissistic emotional abuser and, worse yet, falling in love with a narcissistic emotional abuser, then you have asked yourself no fewer than several, several times, "Why do I keep going back?" You have definitely rationalized multiple thoughts over the process of going back and forth and in and out of the "craziness." "Now I'm stronger. I'm not going to fall for them as I did before. This time I'm not going to cry. I'm not going to be upset like I was before. Just maybe this time they really mean it. For once, I'm going to twist their head around and screw with them." But, assuredly, you were upset again. Once more, you have been betrayed. And, once again, they didn't adjust.

Once again, you look in the mirror and ask yourself, "Why do I keep coming back to Earth?" I know what I know. I didn't grow to love this person because in their lives, they treat me like I am important and special. Almost immediately, I fell in love and can honestly claim they are the love of my life, but none of what happens to me makes any sense whatsoever. I know they're cheating and lying and if someone else did these things to me in my life, I'd walk away so easily that they'd be blown over by the back draft. I know that I am being manipulated physically, and I know that their conduct is absolutely narcissistic. I know all this because I have been studying and reading for years, trying to find out what's going on with me. I know a narcissistic emotional abuser is definitely the one who makes me feel like they're the love of my life. The biggest emotional abuser, but I keep coming there. I have no urge to go there, but I do. "Why am I continuing to go back?"

One response to your "why" is because you chose not to accept what you know already. The difference between what you know and what you believe is enormous. Does a police officer know that their daily routine involves risk, or do they feel that their daily routine involves risk? They think danger exists and plan accordingly. If you honestly believed that by going back to the narcissistic emotional abuser, you were at risk of causing yourself more emotional distress, you would plan accordingly. If you honestly believed that there was a possibility that the next time you went back to the emotional narcissistic abuser that the cliff led you to want to leap off, that you would not have the power to turn back from this time, then you might choose accordingly. You are at risk any time you go back to the narcissistic emotional abuser. Your emotional well-being is at risk and you would choose differently if you truly believed that.

Another response to your "why" is that you want to believe in the potential of man to improve. This person you have fallen in love with is not "all" evil in your mind. You know where they came from and what happened to them in their lives (if what they've told you has any truth to it, though, they're so persuasive that you at least believe it's the truth, regardless of whether what they've told you is true). You hope they've improved. You hope that they have acknowledged their mistakes and made a decision to improve in order to be a better person, kinder and more respectful to you and the world around you. In the case of coping with a narcissistic emotional abuser, a basic fact of life is important to note. Yes, a person can make a decision to change, but as certainly as they can make a decision to change in one direction, the likelihood of going back to where they were before the change was made lies therein.

"Maybe the second answer to your" why "will lead you to your monumental final" why "and, thus, to your" how." "Why do I want to risk wasting more of the time of my precious life hoping that someday the narcissistic emotional abuser will get it? Why do I want to risk wasting more of my life hoping that my worth will be seen someday? I know I have worth. Other individuals see that I have merit.

Time doesn't wait for everyone. This is a part of life. Tomorrow you are not promised any more. You just have this moment. You can choose to be with those that love you or you can choose to be with the mental narcissistic abuser who May grow to love you sometime. As time goes by, either decision is yours. Time doesn't wait for everyone.

How to deal with Illness of Narcissistic Personality

Paying attention to the warning signs is the only way to stop a narcissist. Someone who is self-centered and egotistical is a narcissist. He is someone who admires himself and thinks people are bad in general.

Narcissists often think a lot about how people view them. It is safe to have self-esteem or self-worth. However, it becomes a concern when it is taken to the extreme, such as when someone is completely consumed by himself.

People who have researched this behaviour have found that at one stage in their lives, usually in adolescence, most narcissists have undergone a traumatic incident. The manner in which the narcissist coped with the trauma was to build or take on a different personality. To suit a certain circumstance, some narcissists may change their identities.

The personality of her husband was identified by a woman in a bad marriage as Dr. Jekyll and Mr. Hyde. The husband was, both physically and mentally, severely violent. The husband had demanding demands and he beat her if the wife did not satisfy his demand. However, the arrogant husband behaved as if the marriage was perfect when family or friends came by, and no one knew about the violence. In fact, the husband was adored and they thought he was a great guy.

When someone lives with a narcissist, they know how hard it is to predict the actions of the narcissist. What typically causes the rage of a narcissist is lack of power. When a narcissist feels like she's lost control, she takes out her annoyance on those she supposedly loves. The narcissist can be incredibly sweet and caring and cruel and angry seconds later.

Narcissism in the business world is a person who works well at work, seems like a good, caring person, but doesn't care about others in fact. A narcissist will claim to be a friend of yours but has an ulterior motive. Perhaps you have money, and because of your money, he wants to keep you close. Or maybe you've got a precious talent that a narcissist might use. The relationship is over until the narcissist gets what he wants from you.

There is a fair chance you have come into contact with a narcissist when you think of the people who have come and gone in your life. What's crucial is that you can decide who has a narcissistic personality in order to prevent these individuals.

Narcissists do not like self-confident individuals. They prefer to prey on vulnerable individuals and succumb to the traditional strategies that they use. For a narcissist, people who are shy and fearful of speaking their minds are a great target. Ask personal questions about a narcissist, and if the questions are avoided, that is a sign of narcissistic behavior. As a consequence, since they do not want to respond to personal questions, the narcissist may not be drawn to you.

You would not be on the radar of a narcissist when you exude self-confidence. You will not be a target when you are relaxed with yourself and outspoken. Never apologize for it if you are good. That's a concern if anyone isn't happy with your performance. Someone who really cares for you is going to be delighted with your performance.

Do you live with a narcissist? Right now, you may have individuals in your life that exhibit narcissistic personality characteristics, but you're not sure how to deal with the relationship.

Manipulative tendencies of narcissists. They will exploit you if you let them. But what narcissists do and how to stop people with this trait can be taught.

CHAPTER TEN

NARCISSISTIC EMOTIONAL ABUSER: HOW TO STOP GOING BACK TO THAT END

Narcissistic abuser: forgive or not forgive?

Must abusers of narcissism be kept accountable for their actions?

Many recovered narcissistic abuse victims are grappling with the question of whether or not to keep the narcissist responsible for his behavior. In our recovery, we discover that narcissism is a personality disorder and ask, "Isn't it the same thing as having a mental illness to have a personality disorder? And if so, how can we keep a mentally ill person accountable for their actions?"

One reason we find ourselves in this conundrum is that the narcissist has conditioned us to first abandon our own desires for theirs for many years. Given our brainwashing and our usually gentle forgiving disposition, it is also natural that we ignore our own misery and wonder if narcissists are to be pitied for their lack of self-control.

And where does it fit with forgiveness? If we believe they cannot regulate them, should and should we forgive them for their actions? What if we assume that their actions can be regulated but find it hard to do so? And if we assume that they are in full control of their actions, can we forgive them?

There are two schools of thought about the narcissist's guilt. First of all, I'll talk about the least popular of the two.

Some claim that the narcissist does what he does without deliberate consideration; that his harassment campaign is not premeditated by him. And he is unable to predict the consequences of his decisions or regulate his conduct while he works at a conscious level.

This hypothesis may be valid in part, but as a whole, it is not substantiated, although both theories accept that the narcissist loses control of impulses. And they both maintain that he is not entirely accountable for his acts because he lacks impulse control.

That's where the schools of thinking vary. One claims that his illness is wholly at the mercy of him; the other claims that it is partly at the mercy of him.

The second school of thought is that unwittingly experienced are the actions that drive the narcissist into motion, but that the narcissist is in full charge of how and when he can carry them out. This theory maintains that he recognizes clearly what is right and what is wrong, that he has the ability to predict the consequences of his acts, and that he is well aware of the penalty that others will pay for his decisions. So the decision whether to act on his compulsions or not is taken in a deliberate and calculating manner.

For the narcissist, the dilemma is that overcoming his compulsions is not a choice he is prepared to take. Why should he, then? He cares about nothing but himself.

As far as the narcissist is concerned, only as sources of his narcissistic supply do people exist; sources of worship, praise, and attention. To him, one person does not mean more than another does. People are interchangeable and dispensable; they are merely a means to an end. So if one person doesn't give him what he wants, like garbage, he disposes of them and goes to another supply source.

At the cost of someone who is stupid enough, dependent enough, or eager enough to feed him, the narcissist feeds his never-ending desire for attention. He's an addict who's going to bow to any extent to get his fix. Because he lacks the capacity to empathize, the consequences of what he does to others do not have to be learned. He may know you're hurting, but he's not capable of feeling your pain.

Via inner chaos, conflict and terror, narcissists are consumed. And what do they most fear? They're worried that they're losing their narcissistic supply; the supply they're receiving from us. Acting like parasites on their compulsions is how they relieve the strain and anxiety that stirs within them restlessly. And in relation to their treatment of others, they have no conscience. They don't worry about who needs to be compromised or wasted to satisfy their needs, or feel guilty for them.

Narcissists may lack empathy, but there is no lack of feeling towards them. In fact, while they only feel the sensitivity as it applies to them, they are highly sensitive. And the way other people do, they don't feel feelings. They have a false self; a strong system of protection that prevents them from having to feel their feelings deeply. It stops them from feeling accountable for whatever happens in their lives.

They feel sympathy, but only when it applies to their own personal interests and to themselves. They feel eternally victimized because they have a false sense of grandiosity. They see life as unfair to them; they feel like they're never getting anything they deserve. Everyone owes them all the time, they say.

But should we feel sorry for someone who is ruled by their fears and emotionally suffers a great deal? The answer here is no... We really shouldn't. Who does not have emotional pain and feel fear among us? And we didn't suffer a great deal of pain and terror from the narcissist's side. We are the victims of their actions, not the other way around.

The degree to which every human being struggles is directly linked to how much he causes his daily life to influence these normal human emotions. In the midst of his misery and dread, the narcissist cowers and victimizes others. We are not. In the face of our pain and terror, we draw on our inner strength and courage.

So narcissists have a personality disorder, nor are they innocent people with mental illness who don't know what they're doing? Think this way about it. How many times have you witnessed the narcissist's two faces? How many times have you seen him treat himself completely differently, with different people, under the very same conditions? When others are there to see it, how many times have you seen him regulate his actions, and then totally go off on you when no one is there to see it happen? The presence of option is shown by the fact that he only acts out when he feels he can get away with it.

And how many times have you seen your narcissist with someone they think is important, powerful, popular, or wealthy pouring on the charm? These individuals are the ideal of the narcissist. It does not matter what the morals or ethics of the person are. Their role in life is the only thing that draws the narcissist who feels that he can only associate with other special, rich, or accomplished people because he is unique and special. Narcissists are drawn to rich people, attractive people, and successful individuals that they think will benefit from in some way or who through association can boost their self-image.

Further proof suggesting the presence of option is the fact that narcissists can turn their charm on and off, just like they would a light switch.

And while these people may be respected by the narcissist, he is still envious of them and what they have that he doesn't. That is because, in a state of perpetual jealousy, narcissists exist.

Narcissists are everybody's envious. They envy the fact that there are feelings others have. They envy the homes of others, schooling, marriages, kids, stations in life, professions. They especially envy the reality that others are happy.

It exaggerates their own sense of deprivation and their suffering to be around happier people. Happiness provokes viciousness among narcissists in others. They're going to do almost anything to snuff the light out of someone who's happy, especially someone who they feel is in charge of. They'll lie and badmouth them to others, or do a slow burn about it and then blame or take it out on someone close to them if they can't safely lash out at their target. Making themselves feel better strengthens their sense of omnipotence by making other people feel bad. They make it clear that when they want them to, people close to them are just able to feel good.

For the cruelty they inflict on those nearest to them, narcissists do not feel guilt. They are seen by the narcissist as clear marks that he doesn't have to fight to win over; extensions of himself. He only takes it for granted that they are there for him to exploit as he pleases, safely and readily at his disposal, and satisfy his narcissistic supply as necessary.

Have you ever told your narcissist that your feelings are suffering or that he expresses how badly he makes you feel? Have you ever begged him to stop the way he treats you?

Your thoughts will be taken into account by someone who loves and cares for you, but not so for the narcissist. He sees your weakness the same way a young gazelle sees a lion. It also further provokes his predatory desires.

It adds fuel to his fire as well. He is horrified that you would doubt his actions. He is enraged at the suggestion that you consider everything he does as less than ideal. If you've lived with a narcissist, you know how frightening it can be to be the victim of narcissistic anger.

Narcissistic anger is a method of defense that the false self of the narcissist uses to defend his fragile ego.

But it is also a tool of control designed to erode your self-confidence, bully you, humiliate you, and disable you, all in order to hold you around so that he can continue to feed off you.

While it might be hard for those with narcissistic personality disorder to regulate anger, the motive used to hold you in line is intended. They are well aware of what they do, but they actually do not care about it.

CHAPTER ELEVEN

NARCISSISTIC ABUSE: MOVING FORWARD BEYOND

Whether in the form of parenthood, friendship, a boss, or a romantic relationship, we've all fought with at least one narcissist in our lives. And the encounter still leaves us feeling mentally depleted and utterly drained of energy, whether we have had one or many encounters with someone who has a narcissistic psychological illness.

It is easy for us to note this tendency in certain instances and say "Good bye!" At the expense of a friendship, job or relationship, to that person. But what if it is an expense that we either can't or don't want to pay? What if it's absolutely impossible to reject or exclude this person from our lives because "hey, that's actually my dad / mother / sibling and I love them and want them in my life" or "hey, I can't afford to sacrifice this job opportunity over this"?

Despite the amount of weight that it can take on you, it takes immense bravery to try to make these relationships work. But believe it or not, when dealing with a narcissist, there are steps you can take to help cope and maintain your relationship with them as simple as possible. We have compiled a list of steps below, all taken by psychiatrists and clinicians who have concentrated their clinical research on this disease.

1. Identify the kind of narcissism with which you are concerned.

Narcissism has been classified by previous researchers into two main types: grandiose and fragile. Grandiose individuals have a very high self-esteem and assume that they are superior to everyone else, whereas weak individuals have a very low self-esteem, high levels of insecurity, and sometimes overcompensate with self-absorption and self-centered tendencies. You may take many online quizzes to assess the degree of narcissism that a person has in your life and help you analyze what form they are.

You can change your ways of dealing with them accordingly once you have decided what kind of narcissism this person is. When you direct them to help you accomplish your goals, grandiose individuals can be nice if you delegate tasks of great significance to them and maintain the line of conviction that they are the greatest, while sensitive individuals should continually persuade you and words should be carefully chosen to avoid insulting them in the heat of a debate.

2. Think about their behaviour's origins.

Yes, having to think too much about where they come from is irritating and/or annoying because they are simply unable to think about what their interests and feelings are. But we will feel for them if we understand their history, where they are in their own lives, the sense of the circumstances, even the compassion and empathy that they cannot feel for us.

It might be easier for us to control their rage bursts when we put some thought and attention into what's going for them. It still helps us maintain our composure and tolerance to know that we are the bigger person.

3. Look into yourself to grasp the limitations, boundaries to causes of your own.

Although it's important that you think about where that individual comes from, don't forget to consider what you feel, too. What are this individual's acts and attitudes that bother you, upset you and/or cause you the most? Is there anything that affects you in particular? What are the ambitions you have to sustain this relationship and how far are you prepared to put your own feelings aside for these ambitions?

When you have looked inward and understood what your distress is, you will step on to a strategy where you determine where you are going to draw the line and shape those limits, and where you are going to choose to cope with and learn from feelings. Overall, in times of difficulty, the experience could teach you great lessons about yourself and how to manage your own character. Perhaps this experience will give you great techniques for communication, coping skills and overall development of your relationships.

4. To help you stay sane, come up with a plan.

You must put yourself first in order to preserve harmony and keep this person happy or at least pleased with you as much as possible. This may sound counterproductive, but until you make sure your own mind is at ease and your mental wellbeing is not at risk, you won't be able to form a sustainable partnership with a narcissist. This includes making a strategy where it will never exhaust your patience and resources.

Come up with a plan in which your defined boundaries are respected and ensure that if these lines are crossed, you will follow through with the consequences. This may mean withdrawing yourself from heated discussions to which you see no answer, maintaining a distance from that person and/or restricting those subjects' contact. With this strategy, make sure you remain true to yourself to prevent blow ups and awkward situations for both you and this person.

5. Always, always use a gentle approach.

You need to make sure that the form of communication is as gentle as possible with narcissists of any sort. Unfortunately, you cannot interact as freely and frankly with this person, or in such a clear way as you would with someone else, as they can get defensive very quickly. This is due to the insecurities that this person might have, sensitivities and lack of empathy. When you give them constructive criticism, you never know when a situation could backfire on you because you have made them feel inadequate in some way. Even though it was always your goal to help!

You do not want to be placed in a position where you are in direct disagreement with them, but you do not want your own principles to be undermined at the same time. So, make sure you connect as kindly as you can, so they never feel attacked in any way. Again, this does not mean that when you have hit your endpoint, you should not be prepared to back out and put your foot down, as long as it is still done peacefully and respectfully.

6. In order to face the consequences, be prepared. Once you have put your foot down on a boundary, you must be prepared to be "punished" by this person. Know, this individual would take any sort of disagreement you have as a direct assault on them, no matter how gentle you are about it. They can, depending on the situation, resent you or not. But it's important for you to understand that this is part of the process and that it might mean that you don't get the best treatment from this person as someone else does, but that's a far better outcome than sacrificing your own needs.

7. A sense of humor could save your day.

Yeah, laughing goes a long way and it will allow you to find the humour in the behaviour of a narcissist. No, we don't mean that you're supposed to laugh at the person in their face, but sometimes you can call on their actions with a smile or a joke, particularly with grandiose types. Be careful what circumstances you want to use humour because in a moment of high stress or frustration, they will not understand it. But if they do something naturally, and you're not okay with it, it can help keep the stresses at bay by pointing it out with a sense of humor.

8. Agree that they would require additional assistance.

Depending about how close this person is to you, whether you want a more impactful improvement about your relationship dynamic, you must determine whether or not this person needs an intervention. Especially in cases where this individual is very close to you and it is not an option to keep a distance. Many psychotherapists concentrate on treating patients with this condition, and with outside assistance from a specialist, it could be something you may seek advice on.

9. Keep a positive mind.

Obviously, this person also has good attributes, otherwise you would not even be enough caring to sustain this relationship. Keep the reasons why you want to keep them in your life in mind. Reflect about what positive qualities they have and what you love about them. It should be part of your strategy to sustain conditions where you can make the most of this relationship / friendship's positive side. For example, if you know that there are certain locations, behaviors or individuals that will cause them, do your best to prevent them. If you know that they can get them going with those discussion topics, then stop talking about those things.

Instead, go for events that both of you can enjoy and chat about stuff that you feel that you can both agree on. And always remind yourself, despite their illness, why this person holds such importance in your life.

Uh. 10. Accept, and come to terms with, them.

Yes, in anything and everything you do with this person, it may feel like you are practically walking on eggshells. But it is vital that you note that this person is not purposely doing things. It's not that they're not able to see things your way or attend to your needs / wishes for once, it's that they just can't. If you have to lament the beautiful and fair relationship with this person that you will never have, do it. If you want to sustain it, you must be able to embrace them for who they are, and come to terms with the sort of relationship you'll have. Expecting them to change someday or that you may be able to change them would never end up being good for you or your relationship. You can't change them or the relationship in this situation, you can just change your own mindset and tactics to keep them in your life while keeping yourself as safe as possible.

When you have looked inward and understood what your distress is, you will step on to a strategy where you determine where you are going to draw the line and shape those limits, and where you are going to choose to cope with and learn from feelings. Overall, in times of difficulty, the experience could teach you great lessons about yourself and how to manage your own character.

Perhaps this experience will give you great techniques for communication, coping skills and overall development of your relationships.

CHAPTER TWELVE

SURVIVING NARCISSISTIC ABUSE - POWERFUL TIPS TO CONSIDER

How narcissistic violence will thrive starts by realizing that you have the ability to turn things around. You now realize that continuing to remain in an abusive relationship means losing your soul and identity. Once and for all, you have to decide that you refuse to be a victim.

An exaggerated sense of self-importance has a narcissistic companion. They are capable of causing those around them emotional and psychological distress. When using others to gratify their feelings of superiority, they require constant attention and praise. They retaliate at no end when they are told otherwise or insulted, and will go to great lengths to humiliate you. It is crucial that you comprehend their pattern of behaviour. In dealing with one, this alone will support you a lot.

Tips on how to withstand narcissistic violence are here:

Do not show the vulnerable side of your
Empathy is absent among narcissists. For someone that demonstrates that they are emotionally vulnerable, they lack compassion.

When you readily display rage, sorrow or grief, you will always be an easy target for your partner.

Don't count on a shift from your partner

Your job is not to alter the narcissistic personality of your partner. Suppose they are always going to be this way and it is not up to you to save them. You're just going to suffer even more and you're going to feel disappointment, hurt and frustration again and again.

Establish personal limits

Before everything else, make sure to look after your own needs. If you refuse, they will try to trick you into doing stuff you don't want to do and make you feel guilty. For your choices, be firm. Make it clear you're not going to put up with shouting and other mad methods.

Learn to be forgiving

People suffering from narcissism don't have to harm other people now. Their mental condition prevents them from working with the rest of us in a harmonious way. In order to understand their situation, you are in a stronger place. Forgiveness helps you to recover more easily when you realize that you have the ability to improve the way your own life works out.

As soon as you can, get out of an abusive relationship. The longer you remain in one, the lost liberty and happiness will add up. When you need it, don't hesitate to reach out for help. You will discover that individuals are always prepared to support you. In your fight, you're not alone. You are going to learn that others are in the same boat as you are, too. Be among the ones that are going to be able to start life again.

How to Deal with Narcissistic Violence

When we're upset or hurt, we are all capable of violence. We may be guilty of criticizing, judging, withholding and manipulating, but harassment is taken to a different level by certain perpetrators, including narcissists. Physical, mental, emotional, sexual, financial, and/or spiritual violence may be narcissistic. Certain forms of emotional violence, including coercion, are not easy to detect. Emotional blackmail, using threats and intimidation to exert power may be used. Narcissists are masters of coercion and verbal violence. They can go so far as to make your own views, called gaslighting, question you.

The Motivation Behind Narcissistic Violence

Note that there is a spectrum of narcissistic personality disorder (NPD) and brutality, ranging from silence to aggression. A narcissist would seldom assume responsibility for his or her actions. Generally, they deny their acts, and by accusing the victim, they intensify the violence. Malignant narcissists, in particular, aren't bothered by shame. They can be sadistic and enjoy causing pain. They can be so competitive and unprincipled that anti-social behaviour is involved. Don't associate anti-social personality disorder with narcissism.

Control is the target of narcissistic violence. They behave with the intention of minimizing or even hurting other people. The most important thing about deliberate violence to note is that it's meant to dominate you. The aims of abusers are to increase their power and authority, while creating their victims' doubt, guilt, and dependence. To stop secret feelings of inferiority, they want to feel superior. Knowing this will inspire you. As all bullies, they suffer from humiliation despite their defenses of anger, greed, and self-inflation. Their greatest fear is that they look vulnerable and embarrassed. Knowing this, it's vital not to take an abuser's words and actions personally. This encourages you to confront violence through narcissism.

Dealing with abuse and the inherent mistakes

If you forget the motivations of an abuser, you can naturally react in any of these ineffective ways:

1. With appeasement. It empowers the offender, who sees it as weakness and an incentive to assert further influence, if you placate in order to prevent confrontation and rage.

2. Only begging. This often suggests fragility, which narcissists fear in themselves and others. With

contempt or disgust, they may respond dismissively.

3. Retirement. This is a good temporary strategy for collecting your thoughts and feelings, but it is not an efficient strategy for coping with violence.

4. Fighting and Debating. Your energy is wasted on fighting for the truth. Most perpetrators are not interested in the facts, but rather in justifying and being correct in their position. Verbal conflicts can escalate rapidly to battles that exhaust and harm you. There's nothing won. You are failing and you may end up feeling more victimized, hurt, and hopeless.

5. Defending and Illustrating. Anything beyond a straightforward denial of a false claim leaves you vulnerable to more abuse. You accept an abuser's right to judge, authorize, or harass you when you discuss the substance of what is being said and justify and defend your role. This message is sent out by your reaction: "You have control over my self-esteem. You have the right to approve or disapprove of me. You have the right to be my judge."

6. Pursuit of knowledge. When you desperately want to be understood, this can drive your actions. It is founded on the false hope that a narcissist is interested in knowing you, whereas a narcissist is only interested in winning a dispute and holding the position of superior. Sharing your feelings can

also expose you to further damage or exploitation, depending on the degree of narcissism. It's easier to share your emotions with someone who is safe and cares about them.

7. Complaining and denouncing. Although they can behave harshly, since abusers are fundamentally insecure, they are fragile within. They can eat it, but they can't take it away. It may provoke anger and vindictiveness to complain or criticise an abuser.

8. Yeah. Risks. Making threats if you don't carry them out can lead to retaliation or backfire. Never make a threat that you aren't able to execute. Boundaries with direct implications are more competitive.

9. Oh. Rejection. By excusing, dismissing, or rationalizing violence, don't slip into the pit of denial. And don't fantasize that, at some future time, it will go away or change. The longer it goes on, the more it expands and you will become weaker.

Uh. 10. Self-Blame Do not blame yourself for the actions of an abuser and work harder to be flawless. It's a delusion here. You can't cause someone to get you abused. Only for your own actions are you liable. You're never going to be great enough for an abuser to stop their behaviour, not you, which stems from their insecurities.

Effectively Addressing Violence

Allowing manipulation hurts your self-esteem. It's important to confront it, therefore. Fighting and debating doesn't mean that. It means standing simply and peacefully on your ground and speaking up for yourself and having boundaries to protect your mind, feelings, and body. You must: Before you set limits,

1. Know thy freedom. You must feel entitled to be treated with dignity and that you have basic rights, such as the right to your emotions, the right not to have sex if you refuse, the right to privacy, the right not to be screamed at, touched at, or disrespected. If you have been abused for a long time (or as a child), it is possible that your self-esteem has been

decreased. You cannot trust yourself or have faith any longer.

2. Be of the Assertive. In order to stop becoming passive or aggressive, this requires learning and practice. In coping with verbal putdowns, try these short-term answers:

* I'll be worried about that.

* I'm never going to be the good enough wife (husband) you were looking for.

* When you criticise me, I don't like it. Stop, please.'
(Walk away, then)

* That's your view. I disagree, (or) that's not how I see it.

(Repeat what was said. Add, "Yeah, I see.") * You're thinking...

"* When you chat, I will not talk to you (describe violence, e.g." belittle me).

Leave then.

* Agree that part of it is real. "Yeah, I have burned my dinner." Forget that.
You're a chef that is rotten.
* Humor-" When you get irritated, you are really cute.

3. Be strategic. Know clearly what you want, what the narcissist wants, what the boundaries are, and where in the relationship you have authority. You're dealing with a personality disorder with someone extremely protective. There are clear impact techniques.

4. Set boundaries. Boundaries are laws that dictate the way you want to be handled. The way you allow them to, people can treat you. Before you can express them, you need to know what your boundaries are. This means being in contact with your emotions, listening to your body, understanding your rights, and learning assertiveness. They need to be clear.

Don't hint or expect your mind to read people.

5. Have consequences. It is necessary to communicate and invoke consequences after establishing limits if they are violated. These are not threats, but acts you do to defend yourself or satisfy your needs.

6. Be educational. Research indicates that narcissists have neurological deficiencies that impair their behavioral responses. The best way is to teach a narcissist as a child. Describe the effect of their behavior and offer various behavior rewards and motivation. This may have repercussions for communication. Without becoming emotional, it involves preparing what you're going to say.

Get Support Service

It requires help to respond effectively. Without it, you will languish in self-doubt and succumb to abusive misinformation and denigration. Altering your reactions, let alone those of someone else, is challenging. When you speak up for yourself, expect pushback. This is another reason why it is important to help. You will need bravery and consistency. You'll need bravery and consistency. Whether or not the narcissist makes improvements

Possible Ways To Rebuilding Self-Esteem

You may not know if you have a brief experience with a narcissist that the individual has a personality disorder that is characterized by being very self-absorbed and lacking empathy towards others. When you are, however, a victim of narcissistic violence and are in a relationship with this person, your everyday life becomes confusing and painful.

Let's take a moment to explain a narcissist's actions to those who might not be sure about what the word means until you get into ways you can restore your self-esteem. A individual with narcissistic personality disorder goes through life with an intense need to be praised all the time and told that they are lovely, better than everyone else, and that everybody has the right to only the finest treatment. They easily take offense, and quickly get angry if they perceive a joke as being an insult. They are typically adept at being charming in their desire for recognition and acceptance when they want something from someone else, and then they will have an almost immediate turn into being really angry if they are rejected. They are fast to judge other individuals as inferior and enjoy using words that are racist, demeaning and abusive to other groups of individuals.

For example, a narcissist would generally say things like, "The masses are asses!" believing that he is superior to everyone else.

Although some people like to say that anyone with excess self-love or vanity is a narcissist, that really doesn't do more than offer a description of the surface. To learn more, you need to understand a little about how this condition started, and it is generally mentioned in the descriptions of the condition that it started with trauma early in childhood, during the stage where a healthy sense of self should have been formed by the infant. Instead, as a result of abusive treatment, including neglect, the child developed the view that he was not good enough as he was and needed to build a "perfect" image to show the world that the child wanted all-important acceptance.

As an adult, the narcissist also has a public image of being Mr. Nice Guy or Ms. Great, and by being so fun and friendly to be around, they love (and need) the adoration they can elicit from others. A narcissist usually does favors for others, but still demands returns of much greater favors.

You soon discovered that no matter how much affection and love you showered on this guy; it was never enough if you were closely involved with a narcissist. Although arguing that you are greedy, cold and unresponsive, he or she has always demanded more and more. When you are in this sort of relationship, it's a no-win situation for you. As if you are his verbal punching bag, your self-esteem is pommelled every day!

In order to recover from narcissistic aggression, you must first terminate or restrict the interaction you have with this person. The only recourse for your own mental and emotional wellbeing is to leave whether you are married or in a romantic relationship with the narcissist. If the narcissist is a parent or someone you work with, learn how to restrict the time you spend in their company, and also learn how to set limits so that you can assertively stand up for yourself.

Now, on to five tips to help you start restoring your self-esteem and making it even better than it was before the narcissist got involved.

1. Understand that a sick person is a narcissist. That is not an excuse for their actions, but instead of holding on to the pain, it is a clarification that will help you release their comments and treatment of you. Realize that those remarks in a narcissistic rage were the acting out of a sick person who has no skills for true love, even though their attacks felt so intimate. The remarks they have made are not a true appraisal or assessment of who you really are as a person.

2. Spend some time writing in a journal or computer paper over the next few days or weeks

about hurtful episodes or particular comments he made that keep coming to mind. Write down those ones. And then look at them as if something had been said by a stranger. Narcissists generally make wild allegations and irrational remarks that are intended to cut you off on the knees, make you feel bad about yourself, as if you're worthless. But now what I want you to do is take a look at a couple of those examples you posted, and ask how you would respond if you were told that by a stranger. What you'll discover much of the time is that the comment was absolutely ridiculous! The influence they had over you was in the language of the body and the tone of voice they used, and in the manner in which they insulted things you held dear to your heart. This workout will motivate you to get rid of all those old hurts and just let them float off on the wind. Do not try to replay his words again and again in your head, puzzling out what he may have said, because that keeps the pain fresh as though you were already being assaulted. What he meant was to make you hurt. The phrases were just the gun he used to manipulate and conquer you. For at least a few moments as you cowered or responded, he felt more dominant by dominating you, and in that power he had a fleeting experience of believing that he was 'all right' instead of the horribly inferior person he thinks he is, but he will never confess to.

3. Get busy, get involved with fitness, sports, reading helpful books, going out with friends, learning a new hobby, or cooking a new meal that you've always wanted to try. Stop sitting around

feeling sorry for yourself and telling yourself what's wrong. Most possibly, because you have so many wonderful qualities they are lacking and genuinely admire you for having, the narcissist chooses you as his or her target. You are probably a very kind-hearted and caring person, and that forgiving spirit of yours was acted out by the abuser, understanding that they could count on you to stay and forgive their actions over and over again.

4. Are you breathing yet? A relationship with a narcissistic abuser can feel devastating, but note that you are still alive, and that means that in this life, free from violence, there is more for you to do and enjoy. Part of your birthright is that you deserve to live a life you truly love in which you fulfill your goals and feel happier than you ever

thought possible. By refusing to let the attacker win, you will accomplish this turn from survivor to victorious. Dismiss all the adverse stuff he or she attacked you with.

5. Repeat this affirmation to yourself many times a day, out loud if necessary, so that you hear a voice telling you this: "I do enough, I'm strong enough, I'm enough." Use the power of positive statements to develop high self-esteem so that you can eventually replace those old negative statements that you accepted as valid only because an abuser told them with great authority so much.

It's not an overnight process of restoring your self-esteem when a spouse or parent with narcissistic personality disorder has repeatedly manipulated you, so don't give up. Keep your attention on creating a life for yourself where only caring people and caring events are drawn to you, and soon you will find yourself smiling and enjoying peace of mind and sparkling, good self-esteem.

CONCLUSION

Usually, we become so addicted to keeping them happy during a dysfunctional relationship or relationship with a narcissist that we fail to take care of ourselves. We place them on our priority list first and make sure we listen to their every need. Only to realize that what we do will never be accepted, valued or appropriate for a narcissist. By not putting our own happiness first, we make ourselves physically, mentally and emotionally sick. And this, after a break up with a narcissist, is one of the toughest lessons we remember. We are left with only ourselves to look at after we abandon them or they discard us for fresh supply. Yet we have become so used to looking after their needs that we no longer know how to take care of ourselves. Where will we start then?

The first thing you can do is become brutally frank with yourself and come to realize for far too long that you have put yourself on the back burner. To recognize that the priority should always be your happiness and self-care. You can't pour from an empty cup even to be a good parent and to fulfill the needs of your kids. You have to start making intense self-care a normal routine. Your health and well-being are important. Your quality of life would be drastically decreased without it. Some of the things that made me start Self Care are to take me a couple of minutes every day. I make sure I'm doing something about my own healing and rehabilitation in those few minutes.

Stuff like reading a Narcissistic Abuse book, writing, taking a warm bath, going for a stroll, listening to podcasts or YouTube videos about Healing from Narcissistic Abuse, Art Therapy, listening to music, spending time in nature, watching a funny movie, talking to a friend, painting my nails, drinking a nice cup of coffee, self-care is all that gives you pleasure and warmth. To this list, you can add your own unique items. It would be an enormous step forward in your own recovery to take the time to care for yourself. We have to learn to once again make ourselves a priority. And the relationship you have with yourself is ultimately the most significant relationship you can have. With dignity, you deserve to be treated. So start first by treating yourself with respect.

Eventually!

Thanks for reading, and note that it's never too late: no matter how bad it is, you can still change the condition and get better emotionally.

www.ingramcontent.com/pod-product-compliance
Lightning Source LLC
Chambersburg PA
CBHW061007280326
41935CB00009B/866